How to go
TRAM &
TRAMWAY
MODELLING

How to go
TRAM &
TRAMWAY
MODELLING

DAVID VOICE

 Patrick Stephens, Cambridge

First published in 1982

British Library Cataloguing in Publication Data

Voice, David
  How to go tram and tramway modelling.
  1. Street-railroads—Manuals
  I. Title
  625'.66'0228   TF705

  ISBN 0-85059-564-9

Photoset in 10 on 11 pt English Times by
Manuset Limited, Baldock, Herts.
Printed in Great Britain on 115 gsm Fineblade
coated cartridge by St Edmundsbury Press,
Bury St Edmunds, Suffolk, and bound by
The Garden City Press, Letchworth, Herts,
for the publishers, Patrick Stephens Limited,
Bar Hill, Cambridge, CB3 8EL, England.

Contents

Introduction 6

PART 1: TRAMCARS

Chapter 1   Commercial models 9
Chapter 2   Starting your own models 21
Chapter 3   Four-wheel kits 33
Chapter 4   Bogie car kits 47
Chapter 5   Modifying kits 60
Chapter 6   Research, painting and lining 73
Chapter 7   Scratch-building 86

PART 2: TRAMWAYS

Chapter 8   Layouts 99
Chapter 9   Track 116
Chapter 10   Overhead 132
Chapter 11   Depots 144
Chapter 12   Scenery 155

Illustrated glossary 166

Appendix 1   Kits for British electric tramway systems 168
Appendix 2   Manufacturers of toy and model trams worldwide 180
Appendix 3   Where to see trams in the British Isles 187
Appendix 4   Miscellaneous information 189

Index 191

Introduction

It has given me great pleasure to write this, the first book to explore tramway modelling in OO, HO and N gauges. I had three hopes whilst writing it. To demonstrate to those readers who have not yet entered the field of modelling that the delights of tramway modelling are available to all. To interest existing modellers, particularly those enthusiastic about miniature railways, in trying a few trams. Then, of course, to fire the spirit of existing tramway modellers into making even more trams.

When I first made the move from model railways to trams, more years ago than I care to remember, it seemed a lonely thing to do. It took many years to compile information on what was available, where it could be obtained and, most importantly, who else was interested. In those early days there seemed very little to help anyone get started. I am glad to say that this situation has changed completely. There are no less than 27 British outline tram models being made at the time of writing, with rumours of four more in production and more in the planning stage. Despite this, the most frequent question asked at exhibitions where a tram layout is on display is, 'How do I get started?'. I am grateful to the publishers for giving me the opportunity of answering it in this book.

I hope that my descriptions do not sound too much like orders. I am only too conscious that my modelling methods are not the only ones and may not even be the best. But they have worked for me and should give you a good starting point from which to develop your own style and methods. The other thing which became very clear as I wrote the book was how much I relied on other modellers passing their ideas and skills to me. It is this generous sharing of information which I find so appealing. In this respect I have been constantly surprised by the friendly welcome I have been given when I intruded into other modellers' homes in order to gather information or take photographs.

With so many giving their unbounded help I hardly know where to start my thanks. Malcolm Till has given continuous help during the research and gathering of information. Don Sibley, who shared with me the office of secretary to the small scale modelling group of The Tramway and Light Railway Society, has given much help. I have listed the other people in alphabetical order. Each has contributed to the book and my thanks goes to them all: Noel Dollimore, Michael Funnell, Helmut Gieramm, Bill Hands, Syd Harris, Bill Haynes, Geoffrey Heywood, Alan Kirkman, Ron Lawson, Ann Leedham, Terry Martin, Frank Middleton, Model Tramcar Fellowship, David Orchard, Les Pearson, Geoff Price, Terry Russell, Wally Sayer, Chris Thomas, Don

Two Birmingham tramcars on the author's layout. Chapter 5 describes constructing the vestibules for the Bec Kits used to make these models (model and photo D. Voice).

Thomas, Richard Thomas, Keith Thompson, Tramway and Light Railway Society, Frank Vescoe, Richard Wall, Dave Watkins and Peter White.

For me tramway modelling is a hobby and hobbies are spare time activities. When it comes to writing about your hobby, all the spare time gets taken up. I am most grateful to my family and in particular my wife, for not only their forbearance but also their active help. Thanks also to my mother for taking on the otherwise thankless task of typing the manuscript.

There are many others whose names I do not know, who have knowingly or unknowingly contributed to this work. To all of you go my thanks.

David Voice
February 1982

PART 1: TRAMCARS

Chapter 1

Commercial models

1890-1914

The history of modelling trams began soon after the first rails were laid in the streets of towns and cities. Local manufacturers saw the potential market and, in a small way, began to supply it. One such example is the toy horse-drawn tram made in Halifax, Nova Scotia, in the late 1800s which can be seen in the Pinto Collection (Birmingham Museum and Art Gallery). This model has wooden horses and a wicker-work tram. Individuals were also putting their hand to making tram models. In the Birmingham Museum of Science and Industry is a model steam tram and trailer. Again this was constructed when the originals were running services in the city.

Left *A scene on the South Metropolitan Electric Tramways and Lighting Company Limited at Carshalton in the early 1920s. All the elements of the tramway are clearly seen, the overhead, track and tramcar* (W.J. Haynes).
Below *The Bing double-deck tram introduced in 1907. From the Bing catalogue.*

Above *A tin-plate tram made in the 1920s by Rico. From the collection of G. Price* (photo D. Voice).

Left *The 1934 Dinky tramcar. These models suffer from metal fatigue so must be treated with care. From the collection of G. Price* (photo D. Voice).

When the electric tram was developed and had its amazing growth, the mass production of ready-to-run models began. Against today's standards many of these products seem very crude and would usually be thought of as toys. Since there is no clear distinction between the terms toy and model, I have chosen to use the word model for all the descriptions in the remainder of the chapter. After all, the intent was to represent the real thing in miniature.

The manufacturers who entered the tramway model market were, not surprisingly, also very active in model railways. In the last decade of the 19th century companies such as Carette in Germany and Carlisle and Finch in the USA were offering single-deck electric trams in gauges 0, 1 and 2. By the early years of the 20th century some still famous names were adding trams to their range of railway models. Marklin and Bing in Germany and Lionel in the USA had whole ranges offering four-wheel trams and trailers in several sizes and powered by clockwork or electric motors. Lionel even had a bogie interurban in their range.

Some manufacturers also offered overhead wiring but, in most cases, it was for appearances only and did not supply electricity to the trams, the usual mode of supply being a three-rail system. The rails which the trams ran on came from the manufacturers' standard railway range. For the British market Bing introduced in 1907 a double-deck open-top tram in gauges 0 and 1. With its working headlights it must have been a most attractive model. This was followed in 1908 by a similar double-deck tram in OO gauge. However, this was not the same OO gauge as is now standard. The track gauge was 28 mm (rail centre to rail centre) and the scale probably about 6 mm to the foot.

1914-40

The items mentioned in the previous section laid the foundation for the ready-to-run model tram market and were available until the start of the First World War. After the end of hostilities, those manufacturers who had not ceased trading re-introduced their previous ranges of models and the trams became available again. In the following years the production of tramway items remained fairly static. In the late 1920s Doll, a Nuremberg manufacturer who had branched into railways, introduced a Continental style single-deck tram and trailer. Like previous models this was constructed of tin plate and worked from a three-rail electrical supply. The tram had a non-working pantograph. In the depression of the 1930s a number of companies ceased trading, including the pioneer of inexpensive tin-plate railways and tramways, Bing.

In 1934 the Meccano factory added a double-deck tram to their range of diecast Dinky Toys. This model was not powered. It had four non-railway wheels for push-along play. Priced at 6d (2½p) it was available in various colours and was probably based upon the LCC No 1 bogie tram. This was the first mass-produced British-made model tram.

Post-war years

During the war, manufacturers ceased production of these models, their factories being devoted to the war effort. By this time the heyday of the tram was over. Public and political opinion looked to the motor bus as a more flexible alternative to public transport requiring a lower capital outlay. Those tramway systems which had lasted the war needed many new vehicles. Track needed re-laying and other equipment needed renewing. The smart new bus which had gained from the accelerated technological development during the war was ready and waiting. The model manufacturers, ever aware of public taste, reflected this opinion by not reintroducing their tram models. It was left to other manufacturers to enter the tramway model field. After a slow start the number of companies entering this field was increased dramatically. In order to cover the field comprehensively I will be looking at the supply in broad geographic sections depending on the origins of the prototype the model is based on.

Britain

The first model of a British tram to appear after the pre-war Dinky Toy was in the now famous Models of Yesteryear range introduced by Lesney. The Lesney model was based on the LCC Class E bogie car. These trams were incorporated in the London Transport Executive Fleet. The model appeared in the red livery of the LTE system and, although long disappeared from the shops, examples can be found at collectors' fairs where they have achieved a comparatively high

value. The model was approximately the same scale as N gauge model railways.

Ready-to-run model British trams have been very scarce as there has never been any mass production by British manufacturers. The nearest to this was a venture in the early '60s when models made by Anbrico were marketed by Edward Exley Ltd. The trams had hand-made bodies, constructed from brass stampings and appropriate castings. They were mounted on the standard Hamo chassis and sold ready painted and glazed. These models are no longer available in this form although hand-built trams may still be ordered from Anbrico. The British company then went into production of two types of white metal kit. They were the Bradford Balcony Car and the Sheffield Roberts. Recently a new range of ten white metal kits has been introduced, again to OO gauge. These have all been designed to fit the Tenshodo motor bogie to produce a four-wheeled tram.

Meadowcroft Models also offered a range of ready-to-run OO and O gauge trams made from brass. The scope offered was such that they were made more or less to order, to ensure meeting customers' requirements. These are no longer available, however, the manufacturer continues to offer a range of tramway parts. Sides, ends and roofs, consisting of brass stampings, can be chosen from a large range to make up the desired model. In addition to these parts, Meadowcroft Models supply a wide range of tram accessories which are invaluable to the modeller in 4 mm scale; these include their own overhead wire system.

The most comprehensive range of British tram models is the series of white metal kits produced by Bec Kits. The origins of these go back to the early '60s. Mr Vescoe of Bec Kits had been making white metal kits for the model railway market. Then, out of curiosity and interest in trams, he produced the Leeds Horsfield Kit in 4 mm scale for OO gauge track. The demand was far greater than anticipated and another kit soon followed, this time the E/1 bogie tram of the London system. This was followed by the famous London Feltham tram which was the latest bogie class built for London and many were later sold and

Left *A post-war diecast tram by Johill. From the collection of G. Price* (photo D. Voice).

Right *A Wisbech and Upwell Tramway steam tram engine kit by Keyser (K's)* (model and photo D. Voice).

Below *The tram introduced to London by G.F. Train in 1861. This Varney kit has been motorised with a scratch-built chassis* (model and photo D. Voice).

ran in Leeds. The experimental centre entrance car was sold to Sunderland. The Bec Kits range of trams grew until 18 different types of car were offered. In later years this number was rationalised to 13 by combining similar kits, allowing the previous range to be constructed. All have ready-to-run motorised chassis or bogies as appropriate. The comprehensive extent of this range can be appreciated when it is realised that there are few tramway systems which did not at some time run a tram which is included in the Bec Kits' catalogue.

Another model railway kit manufacturer, N.C. Keyser (K's), entered the tram kit field. They produced a neat four-wheel, single-deck Metropolitan Electric Tramways type E and one of the distinctive steam tram locomotives from the Wisbech and Upwell Tramway. The latter has been immortalised as Toby the Tram Engine in the *Railway Books* by the Rev W. Awdry. Both kits were discontinued about ten years ago. In recent times the steam tram locomotive has been re-introduced. Although rather large for street use as the prototype was built to pull trains of fruit wagons mainly on reserve track alongside the road.

The model is based upon the larger 0-6-0 type of locomotive. It is hoped that the four-wheel electric tram will also make a return to the shops.

Also making 4 mm scale white metal kits, but this time for the bus modeller, is Varney Transport Replicas. This company also introduced a number of trams into their range. The first to be produced was the only horse tram model available in this country. The prototype was the first tram to run in London. In 1861 an American, Mr G. Train, persuaded the London authorities to give permission to lay three tramways in the centre of the city. However, the rail used was not of the now familiar grooved pattern but had a raised step to retain the wheels. This step caused difficulties to the horse-drawn carriages. When caught at the wrong angle the wheel of the carriage was snapped off. In these circumstances it was not surprising that the tramways had disappeared by the end of 1862. The cause of tram transport in London was put back many years. Three electric tram models were later added to the horse tram kit. The distinctive Liverpool Green Goddess, the Southampton Dome and the London HR2. These kits were not motorised and have not been generally available for a few years. However, one occasionally comes across some of them for sale. I understand that ABS Models have acquired the masters. The horse tram kit is available and it is hoped that the others will follow.

A preservation group has entered the OO gauge white metal kit field. The Bournemouth Passenger Transport Association offer Bournemouth tram No 60 (ex-Poole No 6). The kits are made for BPTA by Bec Kits.

A limited edition of etched zinc tram kits were produced by Terry Martin. These extended to modellers the opportunity to add to their range of Liverpool trams. Two types were offered, the Cabin car and the 770 Class. When made up, the etched zinc bodies produce very strong models. In addition to these two trams Terry Martin also offered a white metal supplementary kit. This was designed to replace the upper deck of selected Bec kits and represented the Bellamy roofed cars and the early days in Liverpool.

The latest kit manufacturer to enter the British tram market is Model Tramcar Design. This company is the first to offer etched brass kits. The range started with a classic tramcar, the Blackpool Toastrack and, despite the lack of an enclosed body, the kit is available motorised. The small electric motor is slung in the centre of the car between the bogies and powers two axles by means of flexible drives. This model was followed by the Blackpool and Fleetwood Pantograph car and the Blackpool Standard. There are plans to continue expansion of the range.

In N gauge there are two kits available. An open-top, four-wheel car is made by Cromer Models. This is based on the early type of three-window Brill tramcar. It is a design which was used in considerable numbers by many operators in this country. The kit is not motorised. The second N gauge kit is produced by D and M. This is a freelance design of a totally enclosed four-wheel car which has many characteristics of the new style of tramcar introduced between the wars. The kit is not motorised but is designed to fit on to a Lima chassis.

Tram models have always been popular with the printers of cutout cardboard models. The now defunct, but well known, firm of Micro Models had a number of trams in their range including a double-deck Blackpool car and a London United Tramways open-top car. London United Tramways also featured on a larger model produced by the Historical Commercial Vehicle Club. This was a T type of 1906. By the same designer, Bernard King, but now for the Tramway Museum Society, was a model of Leicester car No 76. The most sophisticated tram car kits produced were in the Trix 1800 series. This four-wheel open-top Brill car was made in 7 mm scale and the kit was not only pre-cut and coloured on both sides but also had glazing and hand rails. The standard was so high that a number were motorised by modellers. Appearing later in the shops was a small Brush tram of 1914 vintage designed by Roy Link and published in a set of road vehicles. Currently still available is a neat 4 mm scale model of the only surviving Birmingham tram, No 395. It is produced by Novus and very appropriately is sold, among other places, in the Science Museum, Birmingham, the home of No 395.

The fretwork firm of Hobbies produced plans for making a West Ham four-wheel tram in plywood. Coincidentally, a similar tram was also marketed by a Hong Kong firm called CM, but in plastic. This had rubber wheels and a friction-drive fly-wheel. In addition to these there are some tram-like items which could not, with the best will, really be called models. Sharps, the toffee people, once put sweets in an oval tin with the print of a double-deck tram on it. It even had four tin wheels attached to the bottom and the lid on top formed the roof. In a similar style, and available in the last few years as a nostalgia item, is a tin money box. Again, it is oval in the style of a tram with the lid forming the roof. However, this is made without the wheels which were such a feature on the Sharps tin. Another confectioner, Terrys, used a tram design for the cardboard wrapping of a collection of small Neapolitan chocolate bars. This represents a six-wheel single-deck tram. Although the general style of the tram is British, there were no six-wheel British cars. The few examples which did exist of six-wheel cars could be found on the Continent.

Europe

The major innovator in the field of European tramway models was the German firm of Hamo. This manufacturer introduced a complete HO gauge tramway system. There were four-wheel and bogie trams and trailers and a special track system to run them on. This system included points and crossovers and was made to resemble a portion of roadway. To complete the range there was an overhead system which clipped on to the track and also a set of works trailers. This is written in the past tense as in the late '60s the range was withdrawn and the trade name is now used to designate the 12-volt DC range of Marklin model railways.

Another on the list no longer available is the steam tram locomotive and matching coach in HOe (that is narrow gauge HO scale to run on 9 mm gauge track) made by the German company of Egger Bahn. Bearing the name *Fiery Elias* this model was based upon the tramway locomotives used by the Upper Rhine Railway Company. Apart from a clockwork model produced in the early part of this century this locomotive is the only example of a ready-to-run steam tram to appear on the market.

Many of the well known model railway manufacturers have extended their ranges into the tramway field. The most extensive currently available is that of the Italian company Rivarossi. They market the only available tramway set. This is complete with overhead, track and tram. The track represents a complete section of the road and is made in modules approximately 8 in square. Straights, curves, points and crossovers are included in the range. Only one type of tram

and trailer is modelled. This is a Milan single-deck four-wheel car. It has a working bow collector. The Rivarossi system is unique in model tramway manufacture as it will only operate from a live overhead and cannot be used on any two-rail system.

Lilliput, the Austrian manufacturer, produce a finely detailed four-wheel tram and trailer. These are based upon the older Vienna trams but are available in a wide range of colours in addition to the red and white of that city. The tram has an operating pantograph but is not wired for current collection. Operation of the tram is through the usual railway two-rail supply.

Another Austrian firm, Roco, were the first to introduce a six-axle articulated tram. This is a model of the 1956 series Duwag trams which can be found all over Europe. The model is available in three liveries, Cologne, Karlsruhe and Albtal Bahn. The current collection of the model can be varied, by the use of a small switch, from an overhead method to the two-rail system, as desired. As this book is written an addition to the range is expected. Based upon the original two-section articulated car the new model will have a third centre section. The whole tram will be carried on four bogies (eight axles). This will follow the prototype practice where tramway companies extended their original stock in just this way to enable greater passenger-carrying capacity whilst retaining one-man operation. The ultimate was reached by the Rhein Haardt Bahn which had a six-bogie (twelve-axle) articulated tram with five sections. Such a model in HO gauge would be 17½ in long but there are no plans to manufacture such a model. Also in the model railway range produced by Roco is a small four-wheel electric locomotive of the type used on the Oberammergau line. This is very similar to the tramway locomotives used by some systems as, for example, in Blackpool. The Roco model has a working pantograph but this can easily be removed and replaced by one of the available working trolley poles.

The British company Bec Kits have also entered the European field. In recent years the comprehensive British range has been extended to include models of

Above left *Very few tram sets have been produced. This is from the Hamo range, no longer produced* (model and photo D.Voice).

Above *The O gauge cardboard kit by Trix. When they were available they were very popular with modellers* (model and photo D. Voice).

Right *The narrow gauge (HOe) model of a tram by Egger Bahn. Alas it is no longer made* (model and photo D. Voice).

classic European trams. The range includes five different Hamburg tram cars, the Z1, Z2, Z2B, V2 and V6, also the Hanover Hawa triebwagen and beiwagen as used in Duisburg. In Holland the Hague has been represented by their 1100 PCC and Belgium by the Brussels PCC.

Also in kit form there is a range of etched brass kits produced by Swedtram Aktiebolag. The majority of trams in this range are of Swedish prototype but the manufacturer includes some Danish and German prototypes. An unusual feature of this company is that they will produce any type of tram desired provided a minimum order of 25 is undertaken.

The German company Gog Tram specialises only in tram models and has a range of four-wheel and bogie trams and trailers available. All the models are based upon German prototypes. The current supply is by the two-rail system

The only tram set made today is this model of a Milan tram complete with track, road, pavement and overhead (model and photo D. Voice).

although the trams have working pantographs. The range is to be increased in the near future to include track work.

The railway accessory firm of Brawa in Germany has a couple of items which are of interest to the tramway modeller. There is a works vehicle which looks like a lorry on a tram chassis and is ideal for tramway use. A set of three small works vehicles is also available and comprises a flat truck and flat truck with wire drum and a third truck with steps for overhead maintenance. In N gauge the German firm of Arnold produces a four-wheel single-deck tram and trailer. This model depicts the MAN/Simmering car of 1909. It is available in two liveries for the tramways of Konigue to Berchtesgaden and Salzburg to Lamprechtshausen. The model trams are two-rail operated but have a working pantograph. Arnold also produce a complete overhead system for their railway range.

The final offering from the Continent is a non-powered model included in the Wiking range of road vehicles. There are two vehicles, a bogie tram and a similar design trailer. Both are based upon Berlin trams. These models are catalogued as HO gauge but are really smaller than that. The correct scale is probably between N and TT gauges.

America

The American market has many suppliers and news of them does not always reach this country. Therefore, this section contains those items which I have come across but in no way does it claim to be complete or even comprehensive.

The American wholesale company Walthers also market their own trolley cars and interurbans. There is a range of interurban kits. These kits use a mixture of materials. The sides are metal stampings, the ends, internal details and trucks are white metal castings, whilst the roof and floor are pre-shaped wood strips. For trolley car builders there is a kit consisting of mazak (or similar metal) castings to make a four-wheel Birney Safety Car.

Bowser is a famous name in American traction. They have a range of kits. In reality these are the least kit-like kits it is possible to get. The body is a one-piece casting which only requires a little filing and then painting. The powered chassis is ready assembled and only needs fitting to the body and having a few details such as trucksides attached. The final job is to fit the trolley poles. There are two trolley cars. A PCC and a Brill Suburban Bogie and three interurbans; a Jewett style combine, Le High Valley Transit *Liberty Belle* Jewett and an Indiana Railroad Interurban. All the kits are also available non-powered.

At the top end of the tram model market are the superb ready-to-run brass models. There are a number of manufacturers and one of the most notable is that of the Japanese company of Suydam. However, these are not within the reach of most people. It puts me in mind of the article I saw in an *American Traction* modelling magazine. There was a comment to the effect that to run these brass trams on your layout you needed to rob banks on the side!

The Yugoslavian manufacturer Mehanotehnika are producing two models of American prototypes. The first is a wooden bodied four-wheel Birney with matching trailer. This model is available in a variety of liveries for both USA and Canadian traction companies. The second model is a very modern Boeing articulated vehicle as used in Boston and on the San Francisco Muni. The model is available in both these liveries. In Great Britain the products of this company have appeared in the packaging of three different concerns; that of Mehanotehnika, AHM, and Model Power.

The American company, Ken Kidder, offer one ready-to-run trolley car. This is a suburban bogie car and is motorised but has non-working trolley poles. These are one-piece plastic mouldings.

From Hong Kong, the firm of Bachmann offer another suburban bogie trolley car. This is the Brill and is based on the same prototype as the Bowser model. The Bachmann model is motorised and ready-to-run but has non-working trolley poles. Again these are one-piece plastic mouldings. Other items in their catalogue which are of interest to tramway modellers are two works track inspection cars. These are based on a Ford van and Jeep station wagon. These tiny powered vehicles could provide great interest on any tramway layout.

Model Traction Supply produce three white metal kits of works vehicles. One is the absolute minimum of a trolley car. It consists of a flat bed with just two tiny dash panels, two controllers and a central trolley standard. Although these kits are not motorised it is possible to provide power by using the motor, drive unit and bogies from Model Tramcar Designs.

Once again Bec Kits appears in the list. One white metal kit is made for the American market and is based on the well known PCC car. This kit, in common with the other bogie kits in their range, has a pair of ready-to-run motorised bogies.

The final offering in this review of American models is a plastic kit of the famous San Francisco cable cars. The model is in O gauge (American O gauge is ¼ in to the foot). This kit is remarkable in a number of ways. It is unusual in being made of plastic, it is the only kit available of a cable car and, incidentally, it is the only tramway kit of a national monument which is the subject of a heritage preservation order.

A selection of modern models of San Francisco cable cars from the collection of G. Price (photo D. Voice).

Japan

In American O gauge the company G. Mark make four plastic kits of Japanese trams. There is a double-deck car from Osaka and three single-deck cars from Tokyo, Kyoto and Osaka. These kits have a particular interest for the British modeller since the Japanese trams ran on the same side of the road as ours. Therefore, the platforms are appropriate for this country. Being older cars the basic designs are very similar to early British trams and the kits can be easily adapted to represent early cars of this country.

Summary

This chapter has been a brief history of the development of commercially available tram models. It has not been possible to cover all the models in this description. A full list of toy and model trams is shown in Appendix Two.

Chapter 2

Starting your own models

Early models

There are many ways into tramway modelling. Some modellers develop their techniques in railway modelling then get interested in trams and make the transfer. Others start collecting model buses then start building their own and from there build one tram, then a few more. Tram enthusiasts who study the tramway systems in this country or who may help at the various tram preservation groups or follow the developments of modern tram systems on the Continent may get the desire to own a tram of their own. The real thing takes up rather too much garage room so a compromise is made with a model. For all, there is the problem of wondering how to make a start. When I made the switch

Blackpool Corporation railgrinder/snowplough No 752 at Lytham Road, a typical works car which makes a good subject for a first tram model (photo W.J. Haynes).

from model railways to tramways there were very few commercial models available. My local model shops just looked bemused when I asked about trams. I had read a few books about British tramway systems and knew a little about works cars. They certainly looked much more straightforward to build than even the simplest passenger tram. So my first model was a works car.

I used the Airfix meat wagon kit as a basis for the model. After that the kit was withdrawn from production. However, after many years, it has been re-introduced. The motor and chassis of my first car was taken from a TT gauge 0-6-0 tank engine. I cut it down to two axles and replaced the wheels with some suitable for OO gauge. Then, with some cardboard, wood and wire, the tram was made. Since then I have had a little more experience of making model trams. New materials, such as plastic card, are now available. So I have built another works car using the same meat wagon kit. It is this second construction which will be examined in detail.

The sides and bulkheads of the tram are taken from the meat wagon kit. The parts used are Nos 27 to 36 inclusive. The hinges on the sides are very much over scale and prone to accidental damage. So I removed them by cutting flush with the sides using a craft knife. The corresponding holes in parts 28, 30, 33 and 35 were filled with plastic modelling putty. For strength the sides were mounted on 20 thou (0.5 mm) plastic card. Two pieces were cut 65 mm × 25 mm. Using polystyrene solvent cement applied with a small, cheap paint brush which is kept solely for this purpose, the four parts making up the one side were glued to the plastic card. This was repeated for the other side. The ends were taken and the curved roof was cut straight across at the height of the sides, using a fine-tooth saw such as a Junior hacksaw or a razor saw. The end was then cut either side of the large mouldings which were in the centre. This centre section was discarded and the two side pieces remaining were glued to a piece of plastic card 27 mm × 25 mm to form the bulkhead. This card backing also formed the centre door in the bulkhead. The second bulkhead was made in the same way. The sides and bulkheads were glued together to form the main body of the tram.

The next consideration was the mechanism. My earlier tram had used a converted TT locomotive mechanism. Since it is completely hidden by the body of the tram any reasonably sized four-wheel chassis could be used. I would suggest using a ready-made chassis unless you are already experienced in modelling. In the case of this works tram I would recommend using a Bec Kits chassis or the Tenshodo motor bogie or, as I did in this model, a Hornby (ex-Triang) motor bogie. This is still available as a spare or can be found on second-hand stalls at model railway exhibitions. My example came from the Canadian range made by Hornby and recently sold in this country. It was a bit high for my purposes so the casting at the top was removed by taking out the screw holding it in place. I took care not to disturb the magnet assembly in any way. In the scrap box I found a nut which fitted the screw and replaced it to hold the assembly together. The mouldings on the side frames were removed by sawing the main part away with a Junior hacksaw and smoothing the side with a file. A

Top right *Making the side of the works car from the Airfix meat van kit* (photo D. Voice).

Centre right *Assembling the body and platforms* (photo D. Voice).

Right *Removing the cast weight above the magnet and smoothing the sides of the bogie* (photo D. Voice).

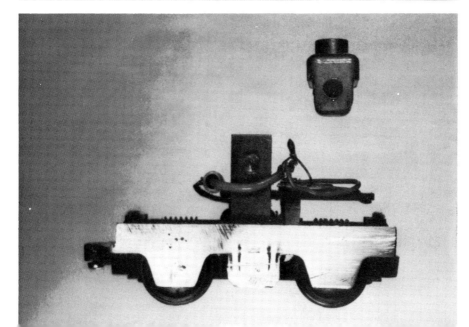

small plastic bag was tied over as much of the motor as possible during this exercise in order to keep out the metal filings. The ends of the bogie were also sawn and filed until the mechanism fitted snugly into the body with the top of the magnet just flush with the top of the body.

Reverting back to the body of the tram, the platforms were then made and added. They were cut from 20 thou plastic card. The semi-circular ends were cut with a craft knife after marking out and the resulting edge smoothed with a file and wet-and-dry abrasive paper (this is sold in motor accessory shops for smoothing car bodies prior to repainting; I used the medium grade for most work and the fine grade to obtain a really smooth finish). The ends could be made by marking out with a pair of dividers, using them as a tool to cut the semi-circle into the plastic. It is only necessary to cut into part of the thickness as the final break is made by bending the card backwards and forwards along the line. A light smoothing with the file may also be needed. The platforms were glued under the ends using the liquid solvent. For strength and position leave the platform body for 24 hours on a flat surface. This will make sure the platforms are level and securely fixed. I always used to have great problems gluing plastic parts together until I discovered from the model aircraft fraternity that all joints should be left alone for 24 hours after gluing. Since applying this rule I have never had any trouble. All the joints have been well secured except on the odd occasion when I have, out of impatience, handled the model without waiting the appropriate time.

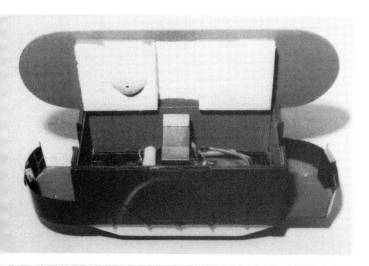

Left *The gap in the roof strengthener to allow room for the motor. Note also the simple truck sides, as yet unpainted* (photo D. Voice).

Below left *Plastic card washers hold the motor unit in place. These will be painted black* (photo D. Voice).

Above right *The complete works car running down the High Street looking fresh from the paint shops* (photo D. Voice).

The dash panels were the next part to be fitted in place. In view of the curve and relatively little support which this part received, the material which was used was thin card 12 mm wide and of a length determined by fitting it to the dash. Provided that the card is of good quality it will keep its shape, take paint well and will not deteriorate under the usual roughish handling my models tend to get. The dashes were fixed to the platforms using a contact adhesive. It was spread thinly over the edge of the platform, the corner of the bulkhead, one end of the card and along the bottom of the card just above the edge. Not too much was used on the plastic card as this type of adhesive will tend to distort the plastic if over used. The adhesive was left to dry in accordance with the manufacturer's recommendations and the dash fixed into place starting at the end against the corner of the bulkhead. If it was not in quite the right position it could easily be re-positioned as the glue is flexible enough to allow slight movement. The card was then bent round the platform and the contact adhesive made a firm joint as soon as the parts were brought together. It was not necessary to hold or clamp in place in order to allow the glue to set. This was the great advantage of using contact adhesive. The dash was inspected to ensure that it was in the correct general position. It was necessary to ease the top edge into the same curve as that of the bottom edge.

The headlights were made by winding some 30-amp fuse wire around a rod of about $\frac{1}{8}$ in in diameter. The wire was cut with some snips, an old pair of scissors would do, in order to form a complete circle. They were glued into the centre of eash dash panel using a smear of contact adhesive. It was worth spending a little time in order to get this most distinctive feature correct. The body was now ready for painting to commence. Works cars are usually painted all in one colour. On my first model I used a bright red. In those days I lived in London and it seemed the natural thing to do. On the new model I decided to use dark brown for no better reason that I had not got a dark brown tram. Humbrol HR142 was used. As is my normal practice, this paint has a matt finish. I find that matt paints are easier to apply and give a better, smoother finish than gloss paints. However, I always finish with at least two coats of gloss varnish to give a 'just out of the paint shop' look. The chapter dealing with painting explores these techniques in more detail. The body and inner and outer surfaces of the dash panels were given two coats of the brown matt paint followed by two coats of clear varnish. The platforms and inner surfaces of the body were painted dark grey (Humbrol Matt 67) again with two coats. No varnish was used. The headlights were filled with white paint and since it was such a small area, I was able to put a large blob of paint into the ring and allow it to spread out to form a clean circle. One coat was sufficient in this case.

The roof was made from 20 thou plastic card cut 110 mm × 34 mm with semi-circular ends. At this point I came across a snag. The magnet of the motor reached to the roof and effectively prevented the trolley mounting being put in the centre of the roof. However, I remembered that the works cars used in London's tramways had trolley poles mounted towards one end of the car. This prevented excessive over-hang when the pole was pulled down from the overhead wire. Therefore I copied this feature and placed the trolley pole mounting towards one end of the car. In this case I used a piece of narrow-bore brass tube which is my standard mounting for the trolley poles I make myself, details of which are contained in a later chapter. There are commercially available trolley poles which would be equally suitable. In all cases some form of rigid support is needed under the plastic card. Two pieces of $\frac{3}{16}$ in thick balsa wood were used measuring 27½ mm (or the exact inside width of the body) × 25 mm. These were glued to the underside of the roof with polystyrene cement. They were mounted on the upside-down roof with the body temporarily placed on it in order that the wooden stiffeners were in the correct position. The gap between them was, of course, clearance for the magnet of the motor. Had a smaller power unit been used the whole roof would have been stiffened and the trolley pole mounted in the centre. A piece of plastic card 32 mm × 6 mm was cut to represent the trolley plank and it was mounted on the roof such that the centre of it, where the trolley pole went, was some 18 mm from the centre of the roof. A hole was drilled for the brass tube which had been cut about 10 mm long. The tube was fitted with 1 mm protruding above the roof and was secured on the underside using epoxy resin. The roof was painted all over using the dark grey paint. Again two coats were applied finishing with two coats of clear varnish.

The controllers were the next items to be made. I could have used white metal castings which are available as accessories from the tram kit manufacturers. I chose to make my own using $\frac{3}{32}$ in thick balsa wood. Two pieces were cut 5 mm × 13 mm. They were painted black with a clear varnish finish. The control handles were made from 15-amp fuse wire, bent to shape and pressed into the top of the balsa controller. The handle and top of the controller were painted using gold, with a coat of varnish to finish the job. A controller was glued at each end just off centre on the dash away from the platform entrance. The brake handle was bent from some of the same wire and glued about 4 mm in from the edge of the dash panel. The roof was glued in place and a hand rail fitted from the platform floor to the roof using the edge of the dash for support.

I had not made a very good job of smoothing the side frames of the motor bogie as you can see from the photos. Rather than spend a lot of time filing and polishing the sides and risking getting metal dust in the motor, I decided to cover them with plastic card. Two pieces were cut 65 mm × 7½ mm with the final 10 mm of each side tapered. These were glued on the sides with the mechanism in place in the body. They were then painted black. The chassis was held in place by gluing some 5 mm thick wood under the platforms on each end of the chassis. A small wood screw was used to fix a large washer, made from plastic card, to the wood. The overlap of the washer on the chassis would keep it from falling out of the body. This is quite a crude method but, nevertheless, is both effective and simple to make. There is nothing worse than a tram which has a loose chassis. You always forget which it is until, with a firm grip on the body, you see the chassis bouncing off the floor.

In this case these pieces of wood were also used as the supports for the plastic card steps which gave this rather delicate item a substantial support. Each step was cut 15 mm square and glued to the wood so that one edge protruded 2 mm just below the open edge of the platform to form the step. All this was painted black with a dark grey tread on the step. The final touch was added by painting a miniature driver who was glued in the appropriate place with one hand on the controller and the other on the brake in true tramway practice. Suitable drivers can be obtained from Bec Kits or modified from model soldiers.

A tram from a trolley car

A start in British tramway modelling can be made by a straightforward modification. The Mehanotehnika Birney four-wheel car is very typical of an

Dudley and Stourbridge No 5 restored by enthusiasts and running again at the Black Country Museum. This tram was the inspiration for the conversion of the Mehanotehnika Birney car (photo D. Voice).

old style American streetcar. It is also a robust, reasonably priced model and with a little work can easily be modified into a representation of a British tram. The model represents a single-ended car with front entrance and rear exit, both on the wrong side for driving on the left-hand side of the road. So on this conversion I started on the body. The chassis was removed by easing the sides of the body over the securing lugs. It dropped away easily and was put in a safe place for later attention. The single bulkhead inside the body was removed, as were the two end windows formed by clear plastic mouldings. The glue band on the side glazing strips was broken using a knife with a sturdy blade and the two glazing strips with their imprinted passengers were removed. The trolley pole assembly was removed by using a drill larger than the fixing rivet. The surface of the rivet was drilled out until the top came away as a neat ring, leaving just the shank of the rivet in the hole. All fittings above and below the roof were removed. The resulting holes were filled with the plastic modelling putty which is used by the aircraft modellers when they are modifying their plastic kits. The small cut-away portion at the bottom of the rear end panel where the coupling link was fixed was also filled with the same compound. Two small pieces of 20 thou plastic card were glued behind each headlight. The body was left for 24 hours and then the roof smoothed with wet-and-dry paper as was the bottom of the rear end panel.

Alternate uprights in the lower part of the side windows were removed using a sharp craft knife. This left each side with four large windows, each with two small drop-lights above. This format was very typical of old style British trams. The cut surface was smoothed with a file and wet-and-dry abrasive. The windows in the hexagonal ends had the cross struts removed on each side but the one in the middle window was left in place. On the side of the end portions all the struts were removed to leave a single unobstructed hole. I had decided to follow the style of the Dudley and Stourbridge tram which is now preserved and running again at the Black Country Museum, Dudley. This is a totally enclosed single-deck car with four doors and no bulkheads. The idea of using the four doors rather than the more usual two openings onto the platforms was attractive in this case as they hid the large mechanism and lead weights used by the

Left *Removing   and stripping down the chassis* (photo D. Voice).

Right Diagram 1: *New doors and panels for the entrances of the Birney tramcar, cut four of each from plastic card.*

Below *First stages in the conversion,   removing window uprights and some horizontals* (photo D. Voice).

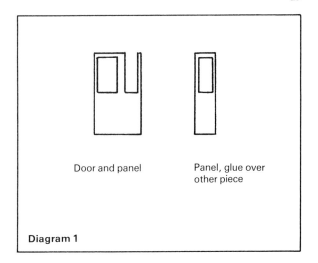

Door and panel   Panel, glue over
                                  other piece

Diagram 1

manufacturer. The door and side window panels were cut from 20 thou plastic card to the shape shown in Diagram 1. The panel was glued over the door section with liquid adhesive. This sub-assembly was then glued over the side panel. The existing panel which contained the door moulding had to have some plastic card glued over the door recess in order to make the side level before placing the new door on top. Where there was a large opening the new door was glued to the frame. This proved sufficient for a secure fixing. In both instances the grab rail mouldings were previously removed using a craft knife. The beading along the side of the tram was added using a strip of pre-cut plastic. This is available in many widths and thicknesses and in this case a piece 0.5 mm × 0.75 mm was used. It was cut longer than required and glued into place with the liquid solvent. When it had set it was trimmed to length using a sharp blade.

At this stage the body was painted. Since the model was using features from the preserved Dudley and Stourbridge tram the livery was also used. The sides,

Left *Fitting the new doors and filling in the holes in the roof. The method of removing the plastic from the windows is shown. Diagonals are cut across the window and the four triangles snapped out. One part shows two triangles removed* (photo D. Voice).

Right *The finished model poses alongside an unmodified tram* (photo D. Voice).

Below right *A Rivarossi trailer converted into a British style demi-car. It has been motorised using a Bec chassis and the trolley pole is from the Meadowcroft range* (model M. Till, photo D. Voice).

ends and inside were given three coats of matt cream (HR103). This was given a coat of clear varnish to prevent finger marks. The upper half of the side panels and the whole of the lower half of the ends were given two coats of dark green paint (Humbrol No 3). This is a gloss paint and is the occasional exception to my usual rule. The doors were then picked out in dark brown (HR142). The insides of the headlights were given a coat of silver paint. The whole body was then given a finishing coat of varnish. The centre of the roof was drilled for the trolley pole fitting. Again I used my own trolley pole and, therefore, fitted a short piece of fine bore tubing using epoxy resin. The roof was painted dark grey (Matt 67) with two coats finished with two further coats of varnish.

The work on the chassis was much less involved. The light bulb was removed and the two lead weights well glued in place. The coupling mouldings at each end of the chassis were cut off using a saw. The side frames were painted in red oxide (HR110), two coats were applied and varnish was not used. The fixing lugs were given three coats of cream and two coats of clear varnish. The chassis was fitted to the body and the tram tested out on the track. As the photo shows, the result is a tram with all the character of a typical early British car. Although all the modifications were relatively small and easily accomplished, the final model now looks quite different from the original.

Other modifications

The detailed descriptions of the two models above have been given not only to show how simple such work is but also to guide you to consider other modifications. The works tram gives much scope to the modeller and another example is the tower car such as the Birmingham works car which was used to repair the overhead on the famous stretches of reserved track where the more usual tower lorries could not reach. It can be made from plastic card and mounted on the Mehanotehnika Birney chassis.

A works tram can be made very simply from the Mehanotehnika Birney car by removing the alternate side window uprights as before. Replace the side glazing and remove the end glazings. Paint the whole tram body, including the side glazing and roof, in the desired colour, for instance, a mid-grey. Replace

the end glazing and the chassis to the body. That is all that is needed unless you are running with an overhead wire in which case you either replace the existing trolley pole as described before or cut the old pole in half and extend it to the required length by soldering a piece of stiff wire between the two parts. This, of course, means that the tram remains single-ended.

A neat little tram of the demi-car type was made by Malcolm Till using the Rivarossi trailer and a Bec 24 mm wheelbase chassis. He removed every other upright to make three large windows each side and also removed the small

The old Airfix Railbus kit shortened to make a freelance modern style tram. It is easily motorised using a Bec chassis. The pantograph is a spare from model railway manufacturers (model and photo D. Voice).

horizontal bars on the end windows. The chassis was removed from the body by releasing the two small lugs at each side. The bulkheads were cut away to clear the Bec chassis, which was held in place by a plastic card floor. The centre of the floor was cut away to allow the chassis to just fit in. It was secured with a small screw through the usual fixing hole. The floor was glued to the body and also formed the platform bases. A suitable trolley pole was fitted to the roof. The car was then painted in the required livery and the windows were glazed. He also painted curtains on the inside of the glazing and added suitably decorated destination boxes using some nice scroll work over the top.

Many years ago Airfix produced a plastic kit of the British Rail four-wheel rail-bus. These kits can occasionally be found and there is always the possibility of it being re-introduced to the range as has happened to a number of similar railway kits. If you do acquire one, it can form the basis of a modern small tram. The photo shows the work necessary and the only extra information required is that a Bec Kit chassis or Tenshodo motor bogie can be used as the power source. Pantographs are available either from tram kit manufacturers or as a spare part from the model railway market. The kit could also be used to make a larger single-deck tram using motor bogies from Bec Kits.

Chapter 3

Four-wheel kits

A single-deck tram

The simplest kit in many ways is the small American Birney car by Walthers. This is not extensively available off the shelf but it is in the Walthers catalogue and may be obtained by asking any of the model shops which do order from Walthers to include it as an item in their next purchase. This kit is not motorised and the castings appear to be made from mazak or a similar metal. The nine parts of the kit consist of two sides, two ends, a roof, two truck sides and two lifeguards. With such a simple array of parts there are no instructions included, or needed. To complete this kit as a running tram you will also need a Bec traction unit of 28 mm wheelbase, a trolley pole, which can be purchased or made according to the instructions in the next chapter, some 20 thou plastic card and $\frac{3}{16}$ in balsa wood.

The parts forming the Walthers USA Birney Safety Car and the Bec traction unit required to motorise it (photo D. Voice).

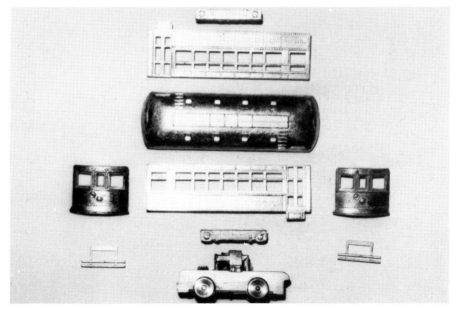

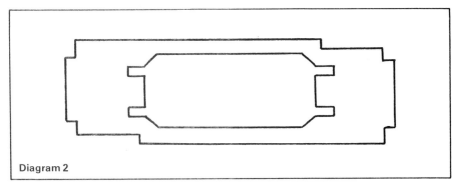

Diagram 2

Above Diagram 2: *Plastic card floor for the Birney Safety Car.*

Left *Floor for the Birney Safety Car and the Bec traction unit ready for fitting* (photo D. Voice).

Below *The complete Birney Car ready to have a run on the layout* (model and photo D. Voice).

Clean the castings with a small square file and remove all flash and casting ridges. Do a dry run; that is assemble the parts without actually gluing them together. This will get you familiar with the method of assembly and show you where any excess metal may need to be filed away in order to make good joints where the parts match. When you are satisfied you should glue the ends and sides together to form the saloon. I used a contact adhesive and, in this case, followed the instructions on the glue in order to allow the parts to bond together on contact. The assembly was placed on the upturned roof, without gluing, and left overnight to set. A rubber band was used to hold the assembly tightly together. The plastic card floor was cut as shown in Diagram 2 and it was checked to ensure that the chassis fitted into the space left for it. A strip of balsa wood 42 mm long was glued on each side of the floor and a rectangle approximately 25 mm × 18 mm under each end. The slot was cut in the balsa rectangle and the edges trimmed to suit the plastic card. I checked that the floor fitted into the body and that, when the chassis was in position, the centres of the wheels were 3 mm from the bottom of the sides. The floor was glued into the saloon locating it against the ledge formed by the raised moulding strips just below the windows. The body was painted inside and out. I decided on a freelance livery as I did not have any details at hand of prototype finishes. I wanted to use a fairly modern style and so painted the whole body inside and out in ivory (Humbrol Gloss No 10) after several coats of matt white. The strip above the window, the beading below the window and the anti-riders at the ends were picked out in dark blue (Humbrol Gloss No 15) using the masking techniques detailed in a later chapter. At this stage I felt that the painting lacked impact so I borrowed an idea from the London buses and painted the passenger doors yellow (Matt No 24) with two coats of varnish to finish. The floor of the saloon was painted dark grey (Matt No 67). During the time spent waiting for various coats of paint to dry I drilled the roof to take the trolley pole mounting and then painted the roof dark grey (Matt No 67) with an ivory (Gloss No 10) underside. Again the matt paint was varnished. In retrospect the overall appearance would have been better with a light or mid-grey roof. The Bec chassis and the light parts of the motor were painted dark grey, making sure that no paint was allowed to get near the rotating part of the motor or the bearings or the gears. At this stage I usually test the chassis after giving the axles, bearings and gears a light oiling. This enables the chassis to be placed directly in the finished body when required and the tram can be run immediately.

The truck sides have a large lug moulded on the inside. This was cut so that only 3 mm protruded. A piece of balsa 5 mm × 13 mm long was glued under the plastic floor in the centre of the tram. When the glue had set I cut the thickness of the balsa until it protruded only 1 mm from the bottom of the body. The truck side was glued to this balsa after satisfying myself that the axle boxes on the truck side casting lined up with the centre of the wheels when the chassis was placed in the body. When all the glue had set the truck side was painted red oxide (Matt HR110) along with the underside of the floor and any other unpainted part of the underfloor detail.

The windows were glazed with acetate sheet, although any clear plastic could have been used. The acetate sheet for the side windows was cut wide enough just to fit between the moulded strengthening strips inside the side castings and the length was such that it stopped short just before the door. The windows in the door were given their own piece of glazing which was glued to the moulded strengthening strip which is down the centre of the door. This does leave the window with a slight gap between it and the door but in practice this is not noticeable. The end castings are curved on the outside but flat on the inside. Since the glazing was fitted inside I did not need to curve the acetate sheet. It was cut to fit inside all the locating lugs which are found on the back of the end castings. In all cases contact adhesive was used to secure the acetate sheet. I use this with great care as it can distort the acetate sheet and if it comes in contact with a visible part of the window it will form an undesirable mark. A suitable standing model figure was chosen to represent the driver. It was painted in matt black picking out the hands and face with a flesh colour paint. Before positioning the driver in the tram I determined which was the preferred direction of travel. It is my experience that the trams will always run slightly better in one direction than the other. This is what I call the 'preferred direction' and it is my custom to place the driver so that he is facing that way. Passengers can now be added to the tram, these details are described later in this chapter.

The lifeguards were glued at the front and back with epoxy resin. A large blob was used to provide a secure joint where the upright of the lifeguard was fixed to the back of the end castings. The lifeguards were painted black and varnished. The roof was placed on the saloon and checked for any high spots. In order to get an accurate fit I rubbed the upside-down body across some fine wet-and-dry paper until the roof made a good fit. It was then glued into place. The chassis

Croydon Corporation Tramways No 4 on the bridge outside East Croydon station (photo W.J. Haynes).

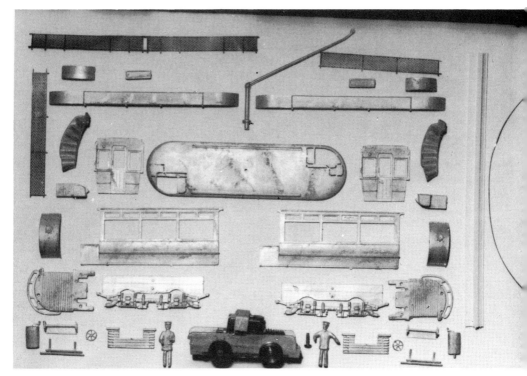

The parts comprising the Bec Kit used to make the Croydon tram, note the reversed stairs required on this model (photo D. Voice).

was fitted to the body and held in place by a small wood screw fixed into the balsa wood under the platforms. The trolley pole was fitted into place and the finished tram given its inaugural run on the layout.

An open-top car

The next kit to be considered is Bec Kit No 3 an open-top car which I built with reversed stairs. This was chosen to represent one of the first series of trams which ran on one of my favourite systems—The Croydon Corporation Tramways. I had a copy of the book *The Tramways of Croydon* by Southmet, published by the Light Rail Transit Association, and I read the relevant parts of the book which showed that the 1 to 35 series was the appropriate car. However, two types of truck were used. The type nearest to that contained in the kit was the Brill 21E used on cars 9, 10, 13, 14, 16 to 22 and 27 to 34. The livery was given as a very dark brown and ivory, the lettering as gold shaded blue. For the ivory I used Humbrol Gloss No 10 and for the brown HR142. The saloon, platforms, dashes and truck sides were assembled in accordance with the instructions in the kit. The upper deck was also assembled with the floor, side and end decency panels but this was kept as a separate sub-assembly at this stage. All the joints were filled with modelling putty which was smoothed after allowing it to set. The majority of excess putty was removed with a file and the final smoothing obtained by using the wet-and-dry paper. The chassis was

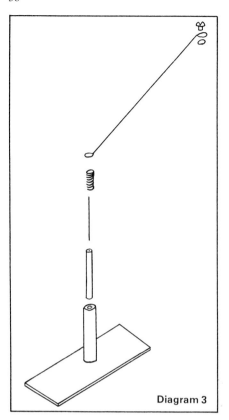

Diagram 3

Left Diagram 3: *Exploded diagram of trolley pole for open-top trams.*

Below *The construction of the upper and lower decks with the trolley standard. The interior and some parts of the exterior have been painted* (photo D. Voice).

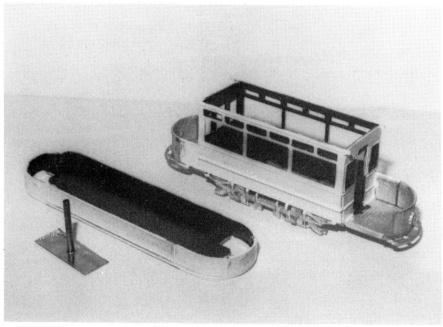

assembled to the saloon and the hole for the fixing screw was drilled. The chassis was then removed and put in a safe place temporarily.

The insides of both assemblies were given coats of dark brown paint as were the external surfaces of the doors, drop-light windows and bulkhead window frames. Then the outsides of both assemblies were given two coats of matt white paint followed by two coats of gloss ivory. This included the inside edges of the main windows in the saloon sides. Particular care was taken in applying this colour in order to prevent the paint going on to the inside surface by the windows or the drop light or the bulkhead window frames and doors. An unsteady hand like mine is greatly helped by using the edges of raised mouldings as guides. Inevitably some paint did get where it was not wanted. When all was dry, these parts were touched up using a fine brush until the neat finish I desired was obtained. Using the masking technique described in a later chapter the upper half of the rocker panel and the inner and outer dash panels were given two coats of dark brown paint. Masking tape was also used to ensure a neat line for the dark brown strip along the lower edge of the upper deck assembly. Similarly the masking tape was used to achieve the dark brown panel in the side decency panels.

In between waiting for the numerous coats of paint to dry, the trolley pole and support standard were made. The design for the open-top car type of trolley pole is shown in Diagram 3. The standard was constructed from two pieces of brass tube each 18 mm long and a piece of thin brass 30 mm × 10 mm. The smaller tube is the type used for point operation on model railways. Although these days plastic tube has gained favour for this task, the brass tube can still be found in either model railway or model aircraft specialist shops. The larger tube is chosen as the one that the smaller tube will just fit into, although it can be a fairly loose fit. The smaller tube was fitted into the larger and a blob of solder at one end held them together. A hole large enough to take the tube was drilled into the centre of the brass rectangle. The tubes were held in a small vice while the rectangle was positioned just on the end which had already been soldered. They were all soldered together and the assembly was checked for squareness. After a couple of re-solderings all was square and satisfactory. A similar sized hole was drilled in the centre of the upper deck floor. The standard assembly was put into place by passing the tube up from the bottom of the floor and the brass rectangle was glued with epoxy resin to the saloon ceiling. This was painted white while the tube representing the standard was painted black. On this Croydon car it was appropriate to drill the hole in the upper deck floor in the centre. However, this was not always so for other open-top trams. Some had the trolley poles mounted slightly to one side and one that I have built, a Wolverhampton & District car had it mounted slightly to one end as well as to one side. Some early open-top cars had the mounting on the very side of the tram, even to the extent on occasions of bolting it on to the outside of the saloon and decency panels.

The trolley pole itself was started by using a 70 mm length of piano wire (this length may vary with the type of tram being modelled). Anything between 22 and 28 gauge wire can be used—although the nearer to 22 the better. Do not forget that the higher the gauge number the thinner the wire. Using a pointed pair of pliers a loop was formed at each end, one of which was a snug fit for the brass screw used for the trolley head. The spring came from a Meccano drive band. It was about 2 mm diameter and has made many trolley poles as each one

uses only 5 mm of spring. If it is difficult to obtain these I understand that Mamod do sell similar types of spring drive. The lower loop in the trolley pole was soldered to the top of the spring and a 10 mm long straight piece of the same piano wire was soldered to the bottom of the spring. Care was taken to keep the centre part of the spring free from solder in order that it acts as the return springing for the trolley pole. A No 2 round-head brass wood screw $\frac{1}{8}$ in long was used for the trolley head. This was screwed into some scrap wood until only the straight shank was visible. The slot was filed into a V shape and the screw was cut off with a Junior hacksaw along the surface of the wood, leaving a small amount of shank on the screw head. A washer was made from 15-amp fuse wire by winding it around the shank of the screw and cutting off the excess wire. The screw was dropped into the loop of the trolley pole and a small piece of thin card which had been soaked in oil was forced over the shank as a temporary spacer. The fuse wire washer was placed on last and soldered to the screw. The oil-soaked card prevented the solder running on to the trolley pole. After tearing away the card, the trolley head was checked to ensure there was sufficient free movement for it to rotate completely. The trolley pole from the top of the spring to the beginning of the top loop was painted matt, then gloss, black. All the moving parts were left unpainted. The pole was now ready to fit into the trolley standard. On my models the trolley poles are only mounted for display or operation. During storage the poles are removed to prevent accidental damage.

The wait between coats of paint was also used as an opportunity to cut the upper deck seats. A simple jig was made from two strips of wood glued and pinned to a wooden base so that the seating moulding would just slide between them. A pencil mark was made at right angles to the strips and a saw cut carefully made vertically downwards with a Junior hacksaw blade. This cut formed the guide for future sawing of the seating strip. A pin was stuck in between the strips some 9 mm from the saw cut. Holding the seating moulding between the strips and against the pin, 14 seats 9 mm long were cut one after

Left *The main sub-assemblies come together and the bulk of the painting is complete* (photo D. Voice).

Right *Jig for cutting seating strip* (photo D. Voice).

Below *Seats set out on double-sided adhesive strip for painting* (photo D. Voice).

another using the slot as a guide for the saw blade. This ensured that all the seats were the same size and the ends were vertical. The pin was moved to 5 mm from the saw cut and four smaller seats cut. These were all stuck to some double-sided tape fixed on to a piece of scrap wood. This made the task of giving two coats of dark brown paint and one coat of varnish much more simple.

The stairs were painted a dark brown on the sides and underneath while the tops of the steps were picked out in dark grey. The half platform and resistance box were painted in red oxide while the platform floor was given a coat of dark grey. The fenders of the tram were detailed by coating with matt followed by gloss black paint. The upper deck was glued to the lower deck and the whole tram (except the platform floors) was given a coat of varnish. The truck sides were

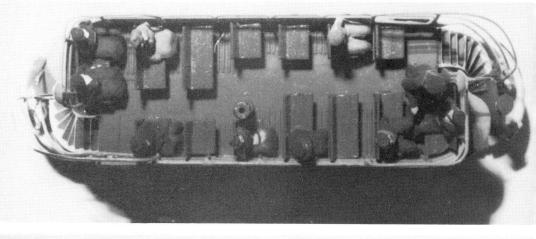

Above left *The top view of the Croydon Corporation car showing the seating pattern* (model and photo D. Voice).

Left *The seating pattern of a Wolverhampton and District uncanopied tram. Note the trolley standard is offset both longitudinally and sideways* (model and photo D. Voice).

Below left *The top deck of a Birmingham Corporation open-top tram showing the shaped end seats* (model and photo D. Voice).

Above *The Sheffield Roberts Car is the exception to the usual rule of 'roof on last'* (model and photo D. Voice).

then given a couple of coats of red oxide. The stair sides, rocker panels and dashes were lined out, as detailed in a later chapter.

The lettering and number were fitted using transfers. In this case the company name along the rocker panel was rather large. I found it easier to make my own transfer using Mabex letters to build up the complete name. This technique is described in a later chapter. Other useful sources for suitable transfers for letters and numbers are produced by Tangley, water slide type, and Blick, dry rub type. The headlamps were picked out in white. Then the panels with any lining or transfers were coated with varnish to protect them. The stairs and half platforms and resistance boxes were glued into position. The wire mesh, the etched brass part of the kit, was painted gloss black and glued to the decency panels using quick-setting epoxy resin. The two side pieces were fitted first, gluing them inside the decency panels allowing about 5 mm of mesh to stick up above the sides. When these had set, the end pieces were curved to shape and two small rectangles cut from each to allow the mesh to clear the locating lugs on the end decency panels. The mesh was then glued into place in the same way as for the sides. To assist accuracy of gluing the end meshes were held in place to the side meshes using clothes pegs. There was a small overlap at the joints of each piece of mesh and this was coated with a small amount of black paint which also acts as a glue. It was rather obvious where the gluing had been done so the insides of the decency panels and the glue were given a quick coat of brown to fool the eye. The chassis was taken from its safe storage and carefully checked and lightly oiled and given the usual test run. When oiling tram chassis it should

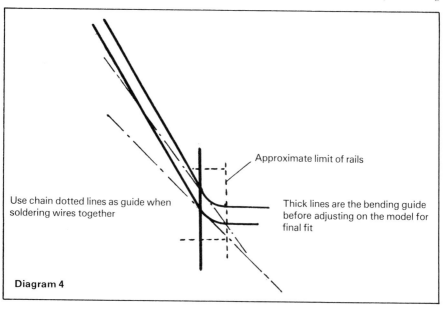

Approximate limit of rails

Use chain dotted lines as guide when soldering wires together

Thick lines are the bending guide before adjusting on the model for final fit

Diagram 4

be remembered that only a small drop of oil is required. Too much may badly affect the motor and will certainly splash over the inside of the saloon windows. The chassis was mounted into the body of the tram and the whole tested to determine the preferred direction. The upper deck seats were then fitted to face this preferred direction. The seating pattern is as given in the instructions. Some of the photos indicate the sort of seating patterns which are used according to the type of tram, staircase and canopy. Had curved end seats been necessary these would have been made from plastic card mounted on small pieces of balsa, the whole being painted dark brown and varnished before being fitted.

Brass wire was used to form the handrails, those on the stairs being made first. Three lengths were soldered as in Diagram 4 and the slanting pieces curved in a spiral roughly the same as the stairs. The two lower parts were then curved as in the diagram. The upright and end pieces were cut to length by trying them against the tram itself. When they were the correct size they were glued into place using quick acting epoxy resin. The top and bottom of the upright were glued against the inside of the dash and decency panel with as large a dab of glue as practical. The hand rails on the ends held them in place. When all was set the other two hand rails were then curved and bent into position by trial and error and matching them up with photographs of the original trams. They were cut to length and fixed into place with the epoxy resin, gluing them to the inside of the decency panel, not to the wire mesh. I found it useful to hold them in place with small crocodile clips while the glue was setting. When all was secure the glue was painted dark brown in order to minimise the visual impact. The soldered joints were given a coat of brass colour paint to hide the silver of the solder. The controllers which had been painted black with a brass top were glued into place and the brake handles bent from the brass wire and glued inside the dash. The protecting rails over the stairwell on the upper deck were bent and soldered as in Diagram 5 and glued into place using the full depth of the side of

Left Diagram 4: *Soldering and bending guide for staircase handrails (reversed stairs).*

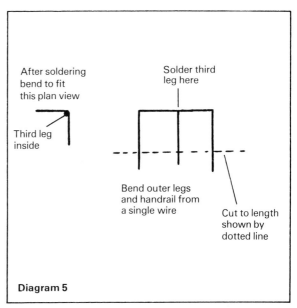

After soldering
bend to fit
this plan view

Solder third
leg here

Third leg
inside

Bend outer legs
and handrail from
a single wire

Cut to length
shown by
dotted line

Diagram 5

Right Diagram 5: *Soldering and bending guide for protecting rails over stairwell.*

the decency panel firmly to secure the end upright. The platform handrail was the next item to be fitted. On this particular tram there was only one handrail at the step and this was fitted on the end of the dash reaching straight to the underside of the canopy. A piece of brass wire was cut to length and glued into place with a small dab at the upper end and using the full edge of the dash as extra support. Life trays, lifeguards and steps were then glued into place and the whole underside painted in red oxide with the tread of the step being dark grey.

Clear acetate sheet was used to glaze the saloon and each piece was cut to give plenty of overlap above and below the windows in order to give as large an area as practical for gluing purposes. The edge above the window was given a thin smear of glue and a tiny spot placed on each upright. The glue used was impact adhesive and the previous warnings about the care needed are re-emphasised. The chassis and bright parts of the motor were painted dark brown making sure that no paint got into the bearings, rotary parts of the motor, gears, axles or wheels. Two strips of plastic card were cut 5 mm wide and just long enough to fit the length of the inside of the saloon. Plastic people were cut at waist level and glued three or four to each piece of card, all facing the same side. They were all painted dark brown, then their clothes, hats, hair, faces and hands were painted according to taste. This seating strip was glued inside the saloon with the backs of the passengers to the window and the tops of the heads about 3 to 4 mm below the top of the main windows. This left sufficient space for the motor to fit, but once in place the passengers effectively hide the motor from all but the most enquiring eyes.

The final details were added to the top deck. The destination boxes were mounted on wire using epoxy resin and painted dark brown with a varnish finish. They were attached at each end by fixing the upright wires with epoxy resin to the inside of the end decency panels. A suitable destination display was chosen from the range produced by Mabex and was fitted to the destination boxes. Several coats of matt black were painted on the driver and conductor.

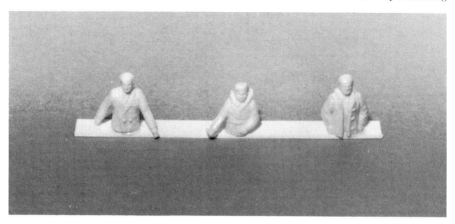

The lower saloon passengers mounted on the longitudinal seat await painting (photo D. Voice).

Their faces and hands were picked out with flesh colour and the conductor's cash satchels were highlighted in brown. The driver was glued at the correct end with the left hand on the controller and the right on the brake handle in true tramway fashion. The conductor can be placed on either upper or lower deck or on the rear platform. I followed my usual preference and fixed him collecting fares from the upper deck passengers. The passengers were the next detail to be painted and glued into place. Usually between six and ten passengers are placed on open-top cars. The seated passengers are taken from any of the OO gauge figures which are produced for model railways. Sometimes they are modified with a craft knife and modelling putty. Having placed the passengers in position the tram was ready to receive the trolley pole and have its first trip on the layout.

All other four-wheel tram kits follow this basic type of construction. Those with roofs usually have this item added at the very end, as explained in the following chapter. The exception to this rule is the Anbrico Sheffield Roberts where the top deck is constructed from the roof downwards. The lower deck is made as usual and the floor between is kept as a third sub-assembly. The interiors and exteriors are painted and detailed as required including all glazing. Then all three parts are brought together and glued leaving a final filling and painting to be carried out around the joints. In order to conceal the fact that this is painted after most of the other painting is done, use the top of the lower deck windows and the bottom of the upper deck ones as natural finishing lines for the newly painted area.

Chapter 4

Bogie car kits

Liverpool Green Goddess, bogie streamliner

In this chapter I will be describing the more advanced techniques used with more complex kits. The first model to be considered is the Liverpool Green Goddess, or more properly the bogie streamliner. These trams were first built in 1936 and in 1953 some were sold to Glasgow where they ran until finally withdrawn from service in 1960. No 869 has been preserved by the Merseyside Tramway Preservation Society. The Varney models kit is currently out of production although it is hoped that it will be reintroduced. However, the style of assembly is similar to that used on other bogie kits produced by different manufacturers.

The Varney kit is not motorised and I decided to use the motorised bogies available as separate items from Bec Kits. Two equal wheel bogies should be ordered. As I had two maximum traction type units in my spares box, I decided to convert them using 9 mm diameter wheels also available as spares. These were used to replace the 7 mm diameter trailing wheels. The solder at the trailing end of the copper-clad keeper strips was cut through using a craft knife. The strips were bent up to allow the trailing wheel to be removed and replaced with the larger wheel set. The strips were put back and secured with a quick touch of the soldering iron. Care was taken over this task (there are hints on soldering techniques later in this chapter). I found that the larger wheel now fouled the

The underside of the Green Goddess model under construction showing the removal of the lower deck floor to make room for the motorising bogies (photo D. Voice).

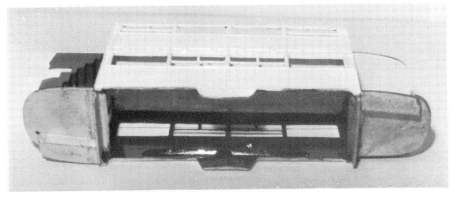

sides of the motor. To cure this problem I removed the motor by cutting through the solder holding the bearing plate in position. This was removed and the motor lifted out, having already cut the solder to the earthed brush holder where necessary. I did not need to remove the connecting wire between the motor and the pick-up wire. With a few strokes of a file I removed the offending corners of the motor casing. It was replaced, the bearing plate was re-soldered into place and the earthed brush holder was electrically connected to the chassis. I then gave them a little oiling and tested them on the track. Having assured myself all was well, I put them to one side in a safe place.

In the construction of this kit I chose to solder the main structure. For many years I had been apprehensive about using solder on white metal. The material used in the castings has a melting point about the same as that of ordinary solder. However, after giving it a try, I have found it to be a useful technique in my modelling. The two major factors in successfully soldering white metal are the special low-melt solder and a specialised flux. The low-melt solder has a melting point that is just below the boiling point of water. So if things should go badly the assembly can be dismantled by just dipping it into a saucepan of boiling water. Although I must say I have not yet had to resort to this rather drastic measure. The flux which I used is Eames 40, this is a liquid easily applied with a small paint brush. The soldering iron I used is the type sold in radio shops—a small 25-watt one. For complete control it should be connected to the mains through a dimmer switch. This is adjusted to keep the temperature of the soldering iron below the melting point of the white metal. I have never got around to getting one and so use the simple method of switching the iron on and off as it gets too hot or too cold. To solder two parts together take each edge and coat it with flux. Melt some low-melt solder on to the iron (this is called tinning) and rub it along the edge until the flux has boiled away and a thin layer of solder covers the surface. Repeat this on the other part. Then bring the parts together and heat them with a freshly tinned iron until the solder melts and the parts become fixed together. I always keep the iron on the work for as little time as possible to reduce the risk of melting the castings.

The parts of the kit were all checked for distortion and cleaned clear of flash and casting pips using files and the craft knife. The upper floor and bulkheads (each in two parts) were soldered together with the lower floor using the techniques described above. To provide room for the power bogies the lower floor was cut just inside each bulkhead and the central portion removed leaving only a platform at each end. The sides were soldered to the upper floor and bulkhead edges. The stair sides and stairs were added. This assembly and the two ends were painted dark brown on the inside (HR142) and matt white on the outside and the window frame edges. Then all surfaces were given two coats of gloss varnish. The handrail on the sides of the stairs was picked out with silver paint and the lower windows in each end casting were glazed. A strip of acetate sheet was cut a few millimetres wider than the depth of the windows and longer than required. Contact adhesive was applied to the window frame by the entrance, to the surface just above and below the window openings and all over the closed panel. The acetate strip was curved and pressed into place. It was held in place with a clothes peg at each end and left to set overnight. The next day the glazing was cut to length. The end castings were then glued on to the main assembly. Solder was not used as the heat would have spoiled the paint. Instead contact adhesive was used. The ends were held in place using elastic bands and

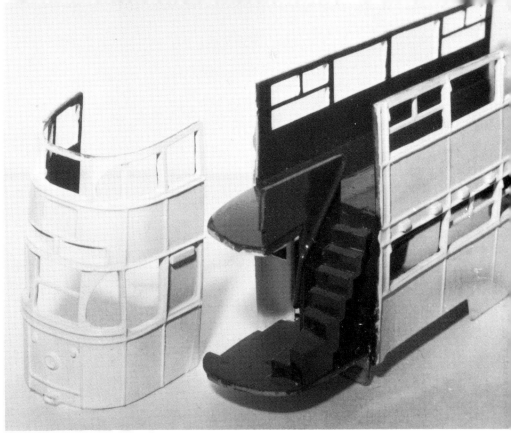

Above *The end of the kit is ready to be fixed on to the body. The interiors have been fully painted and the exteriors given the first coats of white* (photo D. Voice).

Below *With the ends in place and the joints filled and smoothed, the green paint has been applied. The masking tape is being removed to reveal the white strip. See Chapter 6 for details* (photo D. Voice).

The upper deck details are added including passengers (photo D. Voice).

again left overnight. The inevitable gaps left where the ends met the sides were filled using the plastic filler. When set this was smoothed off using the craft knife, file and wet-and-dry paper. The joint and adjoining panels were re-painted in white and finished off with varnish.

A strip of tape was cut 2-2½ mm wide and placed around the tram just below the upper deck windows. This would eventually be removed to leave the white paint showing through to form part of the distinctive livery. In a similar way the lower deck windows were also masked. The tram was then painted green using a matt paint (No 86) this forms the undercoat and was followed with a gloss paint (No 3) to finish. The masking tape was removed and the paintwork touched up as described in the chapter on painting and lining. The coat of arms (a Mabex transfer) and number (white rubbed down transfers by Blick) were added, as were the destination transfers supplied with the kit.

The upper deck seat castings were prepared for the upper saloon. The linking strip cast between the seats did not allow fully seated passengers to be used. Instead the top halves of model people were cut off, painted, then glued to the seats. Before the seating was positioned the upper deck windows were glazed. A strip of glazing material was cut the full height of the inside of the upper deck. I decided to fit the glazing in two parts using the barrier guarding the stairwell as a natural break. The strip was positioned as well as possible and cut deliberately slightly over-size. Then it was trimmed to the exact length by cutting a small piece off at a time until it was a snug fit. When it was the correct length it fitted the curved ends of the tram nicely as it was jammed between the firm pieces of the barriers. It was removed for the last time and impact adhesive smeared along the bottom surface and the top edge of the upper deck side. The strip was carefully replaced avoiding smearing any glue on the visible surface of the windows. It was all held in place by a continuous run of clothes pegs and left overnight to set firmly. Finally, the excess protruding above the sloping ends was removed with a very sharp craft knife.

The roof was checked for fitting and, in places, the sides had to be eased out to allow the locating lugs under the roof to fit in place. I also found that the roof needed to be twisted and bent slightly to ensure a good fit. The roof was drilled to suit the trolley pole fitting. In my case I made my own trolley pole in the way described later and so glued a short piece of fine tubing in the hole with epoxy resin. The underside of the roof was painted white and varnished. The upper surface was given two coats of matt green (Humbrol No 86). The seats and passengers were fixed in position on the upper deck. Then the roof was glued into place using impact adhesive and, when set, given a coat of gloss green (Humbrol No 3) extending over the edge and along the upper horizontal frame of the windows. In model trams the roof tends to be seen more than the rest of the model. This is somewhat different from viewing the real thing where the roof is seldom, if ever, seen. It does mean that the modeller must pay particular attention to the detail and finish of this prominent part. In this case I was able to use the ribs going across the roof to paint it in three sections working very quickly on each part to eliminate any brush marks caused by the paint drying along the leading edge. I noticed some slight gaps between the roof and the side. I filled these with some green Plasticine, pressed into place and cut smooth. The whole roof was re-painted to ensure a good finish. Provided it is not handled the Plasticine is useful in this sort of job. In fact, the roof casting did overhang the ends slightly which did not follow the smooth curves on the ends of the prototype. However, I was worried that I might spoil the whole model if I tried to file and smooth this away. So it was left and, although it is not noticeable, it does give me a slight feeling of irritation when I look closely at the model.

The sides of the lower saloon were glazed with a rectangle of clear acetate sheet leaving the bulkheads without glazing. The platform ends were finished off by fitting the controllers, brake handles, seat and driver. The doors were filed to fit neatly into their space and were then painted, glazed and glued into place. The interiors of the doors were painted plain green and the grab rail picked out in silver. Then, unable to put it off any more, I tackled the powered trucks and the problem of mounting them. In fact, this proved more of a mental block than an engineering puzzle. The main difficulty was in providing sufficient space for the bogies to pivot. I found that to locate them in a position where sufficient movement was available it was necessary to put the driving axles in the centre of the tram and the motors pointing outwards. In addition the shaft of the motor actually stuck through the doorway in the bulkhead. This meant that the bogie support frame could not be bent down at the ends and secured under the platforms. I did try designing a frame using the bogie support castings I had but did not get very far. Then I went to an idea originally used by David Orchard where the bogies were supported on female press studs the next size up. This difference in sizes gives an easy fit and, in this case, I used the 9 mm size (the silver type) which were soldered to two N gauge rails (Code 70). The centres of the press studs were set at 40 mm soldered symmetrically on to

Above *The power bogies fitted with press studs. The bogie carrier is constructed as described in the text. Note that in order to fit the bogies in the body the powered axles are placed inwards. In practice this has no effect on the performance of the model on the track* (photo D. Voice).

Below *The power unit ready to be mounted in the tram, showing the passengers which are used to hide the motors from view* (photo D. Voice).

the two rails which were 80 mm long. A piece of thin brass sheet (taken from the scrap fret of an etched brass kit) was cut 80 mm long and 8 mm wide. This was soldered in three places to hold it secure to the outside of each rail. When dropped into the saloon, this support frame fitted snugly inside the glazing just below the window level. It was taken out and passengers were added to it. Just the head and shoulders were used. The whole thing was painted matt dark brown and the details of the passengers picked out in suitable colours.

Meanwhile, six small blocks of $\frac{1}{32}$ in balsa were glued just below the window line inside the saloon. On each side there was one at each end and one in the middle. It was just possible to manoeuvre the finished support frame past the balsa blocks and then pull it back on to them and firmly fix it in place with epoxy resin. After leaving overnight to set completely, the bogies were popped into place and the tram given a few test runs. Mine leaned heavily to one side and this was cured by first fitting small strips of 40 thou plastic card each side of the male stud on the bogie and then twisting the female studs in the correct direction. There is sufficient flexibility in the thin brass of the support frame to allow this. It still rocked a little on the curve, but not enough to alarm the passengers or driver.

The bogies were removed and a piece of very flexible insulated wire was soldered between the brush holders on the insulated side of the motor on each bogie. The un-insulated side is electrically, as well as mechanically, connected through the bogie support frame. This prevents the possibility of burning out one motor if the other bogie is on a piece of dirt and stops the tram for lack of electrical supply. Then the bogie side castings were fitted by gluing two strips of thin brass across the end of the bogie (at the driven axle) and between the bottom of the motor and the chassis midway between the wheels. The ends of these strips were bent over to allow the side frames to be fixed into position using low-melt solder. Tin the ends of the strips with ordinary solder first, otherwise the low-melt solder will not adhere to them. The sides were set sufficiently apart to allow a little side play on the axles. This was reduced to a minimum by fitting insulated washers. Each washer was cut to remove a small segment. The springiness of the washer meant that the gap opened up to allow the washer to be pushed over the axle and then closed slightly to prevent it dropping off in normal use.

In fixing the bogie sides in place I found it necessary to align the ends of the castings with the ends of the bogie chassis. This was the only way to prevent fouling the body on curves. Even then I had to file a chamfer on the ends of the castings. Unfortunately, it did mean that the axle boxes did not line up with the axle centres on the bogie. One of my major criteria in modelling trams is that they must work with the minimum of problems. When operating at exhibitions the viewing public want to see realistic movement not a big hand coming over to keep prodding or picking up the models. So in this case I decided to exchange accuracy of modelling for running reliability. In fact, the mis-alignment is not too obvious and it was worth that little irritation to see the tram take a test series of 6 in radius reverse curves at top speed with no problems at all. I then felt confident enough to paint the side frames and all the lower parts of the bogie black. The fenders, lifeguards and other underfloor fittings were added and painted black.

The model was completed by adding the trolley pole. Again I constructed my own and Diagram 6 shows the method of assembly. The main trolley pole itself

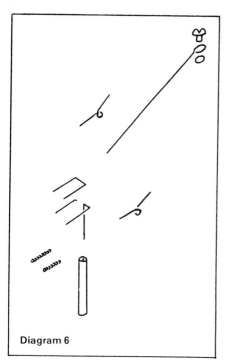

Left Diagram 6: *Exploded diagram of trolley pole for closed-top tram.*

Below *Resplendent in its Liverpool livery the finished model Green Goddess glides down the street* (photo D. Voice).

Right *The completed Blackpool Toast-rack constructed from the Model Tramcar Design kit. This model has a central motor driving the outer axle of each bogie* (photo D. Voice).

Diagram 6

and the trolley head were made in the same way as described in the previous chapter. The external springs were made by first soldering the three pieces of piano wire (I used the same wire as the main pole is made of) forming the fitting for the tube set in the roof and the two arms which support the false springs. The active springing was accomplished with nickel silver wire which has been given a complete twist around a spare piece of the fine bore tubing. These were fitted one to each arm with one end running along the arm and the other sticking up roughly in the direction the pole would take when raised. 15-amp fuse wire was wrapped around the spare tubing and cut about five coils long. This was slipped over an arm (including the nickel silver wire) and soldered at each end. The other arm was treated in the same way. The coiled fuse wire represents the springs found on the real trolley pole. After cutting the remaining two ends of nickel silver wire to equal lengths the pole itself was soldered between them leaving a slight gap by the base. The finished trolley pole was checked for correct springing, squareness of upright to springs and that the trolley was square to the overhead wire. Any error was corrected with pliers and twisting or bending as appropriate. With the exception of any moving parts or rubbing surfaces it was painted gloss black and slipped into place on the roof of the car. A final test run on the layout and the model was ready to be shown to my friends and take its duty at exhibitions.

A Blackpool toast-rack

The next kit to be considered is an etched brass model of a Blackpool toast-rack. The range of etched brass tram kits available is limited and is made by by just one manufacturer, Model Tramcar Designs. These are a good introduction to some of the techniques which can be used when considering scratch-building your own favourite trams and the toast-rack is sufficiently unusual to warrant explanation in depth. The toast-rack tram car derives its name from its most distinctive appearance. The cross bench seats, usually running the full width of the tram, and the absence of a roof or sides made them look like breakfast toast-racks on wheels. In a resort town like Blackpool the toast-rack tram was an obvious attraction. On a hot summer's day what could be better than a tour of the town or a run up and down the promenade with a clear view all around and the wind blowing in your hair? Obviously Blackpool Corporation felt the same way and built many of these trams for their visitors.

This particular kit is based on the last batch of six such trams built in the Rigby Road Works of Blackpool Corporation in 1927. Originally given a red and white livery, the colour was changed to green in 1933. In 1936 a centre gangway was cut which reduced the passenger capacity from 64 to 51 but made life much easier and safer for the conductors. Put away during war-time the cars were never used again for passenger work. Two of them, Nos 165 and 166, were converted in 1953 into television cars. The seats were removed and television broadcasting equipment, including cameras, was fitted. They were used by both BBC and ITV. However, the use of them for outside broadcasts declined in the mid '60s. Car No 166 was donated to the Tramway Museum Society where it was taken to Crich and restored to its original condition and livery. Reinstated to passenger service in 1974, you can still see and ride on it along with the other preserved tramcars.

The first impressions when opening the kit are of confusion and alarm over the multitude of parts incorporated. The brass fret is the most eye-catching item. This is where the name 'etched brass' kit is derived. The main items of the trams are contained within the fret and the method of production is worth explanation. The designer of the kit determines the parts of the tram and draws them in an opened out form with all the bends marked. This master drawing is photographically reduced to the correct size for the model and transferred to one side of the brass sheet which will form the fret. The drawing is defined on the brass by means of an acid resistant material rather than the original lines of the drawing. A similar drawing, previously carefully registered with the first, is used to deposit the acid resistant material on the other side of the brass sheet. This sheet is then dipped into an acid bath which dissolves away any brass not covered by resistant material. This stage is precisely timed to stop when the acid has etched away a depth equivalent to half the thickness of the sheet. Thus where parts are to be formed the brass around them has been etched from both sides and entirely removed. Bend lines and finely detailed representation are etched on one side only and thus penetrate half the thickness of the material. Everything is held in place by leaving small support pieces bridging the gap from the item to the main fret. This also has numbers etched into it to identify the parts. In the case of the toast-rack there are no less than 106 parts contained in the fret.

In addition the kit has a number of other items such as a turned brass trolley standard, trolley pole, ready assembled bogies, motor and other parts for the driving mechanism, headlamps, white metal controllers, destination boxes and fender castings. The golden rule with all such kits is to leave them on the fret or in the bag or box until you need them. Where a kit does not have a ready-to-run chassis I prefer to build the mechanism first in order that my subsequent assembly of the body can be adjusted to ensure that the height of the tram is kept correct. In this particular case, there were no complications of this sort but nevertheless I started with the chassis. The bogies and motor were to be mounted on a false floor so this was the first item to be taken from the fret. I cut through the support pieces with a small pair of wire cutters and then, using a fine file, smoothed the remaining spigots off the edge of the piece.

The instructions recommended bolting the motor support box in place, in fact I soldered it in. The solder used on all the brass parts was ordinary solder and I used the technique which I have found most successful over the years. The two parts to be joined were given a smear of flux paste (I used Fluxite). The parts were then tinned. This is achieved by melting a small amount of solder on to the solder iron and then smearing it over the required area of the part. The parts were joined by melting another small part of solder on to the iron and running it along the joint while holding the parts together in the required position. This was best achieved by laying one part on a smooth piece of scrap wood and holding the other with pliers or tweezers. I must admit that often I just hold the bits with my fingers and I have the burn scars to prove it.

The motor was held in the box while it was soldered together. This is one of the times when the tinning shows its great advantages. The parts were tinned away from the motor so that when it was in place a quick touch of the soldering iron fixed everything firmly. Very little heat got to the motor and, therefore, it was not burned. Where the solder did not take to the joint at the first attempt I let the whole thing cool down before trying again. Had the soldering iron been allowed to linger on the box too long there would have been danger of doing permanent harm to the small motor. The false floor was bent to shape and soldered with the motor also being fitted. The bogie stirrups were bolted into place using the insulating washers and plastic card. I found it useful to cover the side parts of the stirrup with adhesive tape to ensure that no short circuits were caused by the insulated wheel accidentally touching it. Otherwise the mechanism was made up according to the instructions. The adjustment of the bogies and flexible drive was critical for the maximum performance. I tested the chassis on the track and checked first for any slipping of the driven wheels. This did occur so the bogies were removed from the stirrups and with a small pair of long-nosed pliers the stirrup support plate was eased so that it tipped down towards the end of the tram and up towards the middle. This put more weight on to the driven axles. The bogies were re-assembled and given another run. I checked carefully to ensure that the non-driven wheels were not tending to climb up the rails and jump off the track. If this had happened I would have eased the stirrup support plate to less of an angle. The length of the flexible drive was carefully checked. When stationary on straight track there was a little backwards and forwards play on the worm shaft as the flexible drive was moved with a cocktail stick.

Attention was now turned to the body of the tram. Again the instructions were followed but with some minor modifications. In view of the heat required to solder the trolley standard into the floor this was the first part of the assembly undertaken. It took a couple of tries before I got it sufficiently vertical to satisfy myself. Then the long seats were soldered into place keeping the solder hidden on the underside of the floor. The small seats either side of the standard were bent to shape and then a vertical support was soldered to the inner edge of the seat before locating it into the floor. This was to overcome the problem of getting the soldering iron past the standard when the seat was in position. The

remainder of the seat supports were tinned on one side while they were still on the fret. This prevented any problems of how to hold the tiny pieces. The seat sides were given a coat of Fluxite and the supports were soldered in place by holding with a pair of pointed tweezers in the correct position on the seat side and then touching with the iron until the heat had penetrated the support, melted the solder which, in turn, evaporated the flux and adhered to the seat side. The most difficult part was not removing the tweezers while I waited the few seconds for the solder to cool and solidify. By the time I was halfway along the second side I was quite proficient at it. The end tags of the seat backs were all tinned on the fret and then each back was removed and bent to shape. A small jig was used to get the seat back into the correct position. With one hand on the jig and the other on the soldering iron I had to rely on the spring in the supports to hold the backs in position. This they did for sufficient time to touch the iron on the joint and run the two sets of tinning to form a strong joint.

The rest of the model was straightforward. I used low-melt solder to fix the white metal castings into place although epoxy resin would also have been suitable. The chassis and body were fixed together with epoxy resin using a large blob at each end and the centre.

Painting this model was simpler than I had expected. The whole thing was first given a coat of self-etching primer. This should always be used on any brass parts as without it the paint is very prone to chipping off under the slightest knock. The remainder of the tram was painted using a coloured postcard of the preserved vehicle at Crich as a guide. I also had some detail photos which I had taken on an earlier visit to the Museum. When the painting was finished and the tram had been given a coat of varnish the grab rails were fitted. These were fixed in position using small touches of quick acting epoxy resin. One side was done at a time to allow the grab rails to lie horizontally undisturbed until the resin had set. Finally the seat sides and grab rails were given another coat of varnish to protect the natural brass finish of the rails. As is my usual practice, a few passengers were added. These come from the very nicely detailed Ratio range of white metal figures.

When running in the layout the toast-rack really does create a sensation. The inconspicuous underslung motor and the delicate appearance of the etched brass all combine to create a most attractive tram. When I first built the toast-rack, I felt that the mechanism could have other uses. I managed to get one of the non-powered American Modern Traction Company kits of a flat-bed works car. This seemed an ideal way of trying the mechanism. A spare set of parts was obtained from the manufacturer and it was very simple to adapt the white metal casting to take the motor and bogies. This now gives the absolute bare minimum of tram, just a floor, trolley standard, two small dashes and a driver.

Top left *The jig for setting the backs of the seats on the toast-rack tram* (photo D. Voice).

Centre left *The setting jig in place. It is held in place with one hand while the other is used to solder the seat back in place* (photo D. Voice).

Left *A detail close-up of the finished toast-rack showing the slight rake to the seat backs* (photo D. Voice).

Chapter 5

Modifying kits

Kits do not always exactly fit the prototype being modelled. In these cases it may be possible to modify or adapt the kit to suit and some are examined in this chapter.

Vestibules

Though the problem of building vestibule cars has been reduced by the introduction of the new range of Anbrico kits, you may find that it would be easier to add a vestibule to a Bec kit rather than do other modifications to the Anbrico kits. This is a task which may put off the kit builder but, in fact, is not all that difficult. The kit should be built as described in the previous chapters and can even be painted out if desired. The only point to take into account is not to place the staircase controller or handbrake in position until after the vestibule and its glazing have been fitted.

Using a strip of paper wrapped around the top edge of the dash, pencil marks can be made to locate the ends of the dash and the point at which the curvature starts. When taken off, the paper gives the true length of the dash. These dimensions should be transferred to a drawing. The verticals at the ends of the line can be drawn with another horizontal at the height of the underside of the canopy. From photographs or drawings of the prototype determine the position of the remaining upright pillars. Here it may be necessary to modify the precise position in order to accommodate the curvature which is already built into the model. This is why the mark locating the start of the curve is so important. If

Left *The construction technique used in this chapter and Chapter 7 is demonstrated by this dash and vestibule sub-assembly* (model and photo D. Orchard).

Right *Close-up of the finished vestibule, showing the distinctive Birmingham features. This modification completely transforms the appearance of these kits* (model and photo D. Voice).

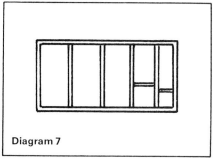

Diagram 7

Above *Sunderland 100, this is how the experimental centre entrance Feltham (MET No 331) finished its working life. The trolley poles were replaced by a pantograph and it was given a new livery. This tram can be seen awaiting restoration at Crich to begin a new lease of life carrying passengers at the National Tramway Museum* (photo D. Voice collection).

Left Diagram 7: *Negative drawing of vestibule to convert a Bec Kit to a Birmingham car.*

there is a slope inwards on the screens at the front, use the bottom horizontal for all the marking out. The complication of slopes will be attended to later. Do not forget to allow for the width of the window frames in the drawing. When it is finished tape it to a window with the drawing facing outwards. Trace over another sheet of paper to produce an exact 'negative' drawing. An example is shown in Diagram 7. Repeat for a second negative. Now call in at your local model shop (or buy by mail from shops advertising in the model railway Press) and obtain nickel silver or brass strip of the appropriate width (1 mm or 1½ mm) for the frames. The material should be 10 thou thick. This is often sold under the term 'boiler banding'. The length should be much more than the total framework as calculated from the two drawings. It is not an expensive item and the spare which may be left is always useful at a later occasion. Tape one of the negative drawings to a flat piece of scrap wood. Cut two pieces of the metal strip to the length of the horizontals and attach these to the drawing in the appropriate places using small pieces of sticky tape. Cut the verticals to length, they should be long enough to rest on the horizontals but not to overlap them. Position the end vertical which will be against the bulkhead (this will be the left-hand one on the drawing). Solder it to the two horizontals.

Now it should be clear why a negative drawing is used. All the soldering is carried out on what will be the inside of the vestibule. Therefore, the overlap of the framing and any fillets of solder will be quite inconspicuous when all is fitted in place. Continue soldering the remaining uprights in place. If the vestibule has a sloping front, leave the top joints free from solder except for the uprights which will be along the flat side of the dash. Remove the assembly from the drawing and, using the model tram as a guide, bend the framework to fit the

The new sides are mated with the kit ends. The soldered construction of the sides can be seen, as can the rail used for stiffening and the Milliput securing the ends (photo D. Voice).

dash and canopy. Check that the uprights are in the correct place. If not, unsolder and reposition them. Amend the second drawing as necessary. When all looks well, the tops of the sloping uprights can be soldered into place (well away from the white metal model) and the top of the framework can be trimmed to length. Any other details such as metal plates, horizontal bars and so on can now be added. For example, on Birmingham cars there was a most distinctive curved plate on the lower part of the window nearest the entrance. This feature can be made from thin sheet metal. In view of the possibility of accidentally melting previously soldered joints on the delicate framework, I recommend gluing these extra parts in place. Epoxy resin is ideal for such a job. The second vestibule can now be made in the same way using the other drawing. When all is complete the vestibules can be glued into place ready for painting and glazing. The glazing strip should be cut as deep as possible without obstructing any mouldings on the inside of the dash. Keep trying it in the model until you are satisfied with the fit. Smear contact adhesive along the top edge and bottom surface and push it into place to fit the curve of the dash. Hold the glazing strip in the correct position by using a clothes peg and leave it over-night for the glue to set firmly. Then, if necessary, trim the glazing strip to length. The stairs, controller and hand brake should then be fitted and these will effectively hide the method which you have used to glaze the model.

Metropolitan Electric Tramways No 331

No 331 in the Metropolitan Electric Tramways fleet was the last experimental tram to be built prior to the construction of the Feltham Class. In 1901 the Union Construction Company was set up by the 'Underground' consortium, which included London United and MET, to construct underground railway stock. Later a new range of tramcars was built and then the first trolley buses to run in London were completed. In the search for a new tramcar design a number of prototypes were constructed to try out a variety of features. The first was No 318 in the MET fleet and was more popularly known as *Bluebell* from the distinctive livery. The next experimental car was *Poppy*, No 350, in the LUT fleet. From the lessons learnt Nos 320 and 330 were constructed using a new

Above left *The body has been fully painted, lined and given transfers. It now awaits glazing, interior details, roof and bogies* (photo D. Voice).

Left *The finished model showing that the fabricated metal sides do not look out of place with the cast kit parts* (photo D. Voice).

Above *Metropolitan Electric Tramways 331 ready for service and looking fresh from the paint shops* (model and photo D. Voice).

body design. Although visually very similar, No 320 was mounted on equal wheel bogies while No 330 had maximum traction bogies. These trams directly led to the Feltham Class of cars which were slightly different from the two prototypes, mainly in the height of the cab in relation to the lower saloon. One last prototype was constructed a few months ahead of the main class. It was in outline the same as the new Feltham Class, however, instead of having rear entrance and front exit, No 331 (nicknamed *Cissie*) had a centre entrance/exit. This gave a completely new look to the side of the vehicle even to the extent of having a different arrangement of upper saloon windows. In order to allow easy access to the tram, the floor in the centre was lower than in the saloons. The side panels curved down to form the entrance. The stairs were situated by each entrance and it was intended that the conductor would stay in the centre well and collect fares as passengers got on. It was a form of pay-as-you-enter scheme. This idea was abandoned when the vehicle actually entered service. No doubt the fears of delays caused by passengers being prevented from boarding while the fares were taken over-ruled this experiment. Otherwise the tram saw worthwhile use on the Metropolitan system until the companies were absorbed into the London Transport Executive in 1933.

No 331 joined the new combined fleet to become LTE No 2168. At this time the major disadvantage of the design, for the London system, became apparent. The low platform in the centre of the car prevented a plough carrier from being

Above *A comparison of standard Feltham No 371, a straight construction of the Bec Kit, with the centre entrance car No 331* (model and photo D. Voice).

Above right Diagram 8: *Negative drawing of the side of prototype Feltham No 331.*

fitted. This stopped the tram from travelling on to the central LCC system and hence reaching the City centre terminals. The experimental car just could not fit into the new LTE policies and so it was sold. The buyer was Sunderland Corporation who numbered it 100, removed the trolley poles and fitted their usual pantograph. It ran in Sunderland until 1952, when it was sold, although it stayed in the city until the system closed in 1954. However, this was not the end for this unique tram. An enthusiast had bought it and, after several moves, as appropriate storage was sought, it found a permanent home in the Tramway Museum at Crich, where it can be seen today. There are also other surviving Felthams; MET No 355 (LTE No 2099 and later Leeds No 501) is on show in the London Transport Collection, Covent Garden. If you can make it to the Seashore Electric Railway Museum, America, there is another preserved Feltham. MET No 341 (LTE No 2085, Leeds No 526).

There is a kit made by Bec for the standard Feltham tram and this can be modified surprisingly easily into the centre entrance No 331 car. All the dimensions of No 331 externally match the standard tram, although the sides are quite different in layout. The whole kit can be used with no alteration other than a slight change on the bogies and, of course, new sides. This kit is probably best ordered direct from the manufacturer as equal wheel bogies can be ordered in place of the maximum traction type normally supplied with the kit. In my case I already had the standard kit before deciding to make the modification. So I ordered the appropriate 9 mm diameter wheel sets from Bec kits and, when they arrived, swopped them for the smaller maximum traction trailing wheels. I cut through the spots of solder securing the copper-clad keeper strips at the trailing end with a craft knife. They were levered up enough to slip the unwanted axle out and the new one in. Then, after having been pushed back

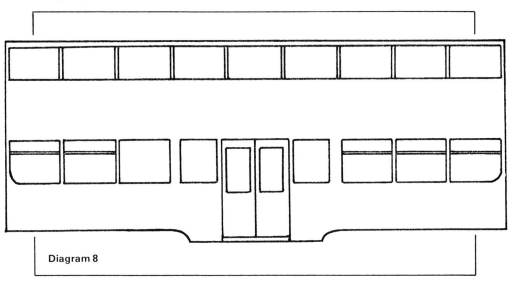

Diagram 8

into place, a touch of ordinary solder on each end secured everything. The next job was to construct the new sides of the tram. I obtained a few photos of No 331 and also found some pictures in books about London's trams. From these it was a simple matter to draw the side out. Diagram 8 gives the negative drawing but I will describe the method in case you wish to do a similar modification on a different kit.

The new side must be the same outside dimensions as that replaced so the drawing starts with the outer lines. Then the vertical dimensions are marked off. That is the upper and lower horizontals for the windows and the doorway. These can be scaled from a clear photo using the formula: scale dimension equals distance on photo times scale height divided by height on photo. A pocket calculator can make the job easier. The only rule is that if the photo is not absolutely side on, keep your measurements in the same vertical plane otherwise the perspective will give you wrong answers. If you have got a good side view the same technique can be used to mark out the window and other widths. If not you may have to do a bit of trial and error until the drawing looks right. Of course, if you can get a proper drawing and perhaps visit the prototype at Crich you will get better accuracy.

Anyway, when satisfied with the drawing take two 'negative' drawings as described previously. Actually for No 331 the only difference between positive and negative is in the lower saloon window opening bars.

Having completed this job myself I taped one drawing to a piece of scrap plywood. I had already purchased some 1½ mm wide 10 thou nickel silver strip and a sheet of 10 thou nickel silver. The sheet was marked out and cut to form the horizontal side pieces between the two sets of windows and below the lower deck windows. There was a choice of two methods of cutting these strips. I could have used shears (which I have not got) or a pair of scissors kept purely to act as shears (which I have got). Since metal tends to curl when cut this way, there was a special method to use. The first cut should be made some ½ in from the final line. The scrap section left should be cut again half-way between the edge and the finished line. This should be repeated until the line can be reached

The same conversion, but a different modeller. David Orchard made this version of No 331 in its London Transport days. It was eventually numbered 2168, but was soon sold to Sunderland (model and photo D. Orchard).

by cutting a narrow section. By this means the twisting and curling forces are all absorbed by strips cut away leaving the main piece relatively free. It may need a slight adjustment to regain its flatness.

However, in this case I chose to use the other method where the sheet is cut along the finish line using a razor saw. Thin sheet metal is not the best of materials to saw and some special precautions were taken. The sheet was taped firmly to some scrap plywood so that the cutting line was 1 or 2 mm over the edge. This gave firm support along the cut and avoided buckling the metal. The sawing was done gently and with plenty of resting when I felt things were either getting tiring or frustrating. Actually it did not take long to cut it all out and a quick rub with a fine file smoothed the edge leaving the parts the correct size. The curve and inset lower edge was formed by cutting with the scissors in the way described, leaving some waste material by the curve. This was then filed away with a round file until the curve was formed. When filing the thin sheet it was kept on a piece of wood leaving just a few millimetres over the edge where the filing was taking place. Again this firm support avoided accidental kinking of the metal. At this stage I was anticipating forming the prominent curve on the lower deck windows by filling the corner with solder and filing to shape. In fact this did not work and I had to cut small plastic card shapes and glue them into place when all else was finished. So if you are planning to make No 331 I suggest you incorporate that curve into the side panels as you cut them out.

The main side panels were taped to the drawing as was the top horizontal of the upper deck windows. Verticals for the windows were cut from the 1½ mm strip with two extra 3 mm wide strips for the lower deck. The side panels were tinned where the verticals were to go. Each vertical was given a smear of flux then placed in the correct position and fixed by applying the soldering iron until the solder tinning melted and adhered to the strip. All the verticals were soldered in this way. The door was also soldered into place constructing it in the same way using a piece cut from the sheet for the lower panel and strip for the windows. A strengthening bar of code 80 (N gauge) rail was soldered along the upper panel where the floor was to be. This not only held the side straight and gave it stiffness, it also acted as the support for the floor when it was fitted. After all this the side appeared to be twisted and this was cured by re-soldering some of the uprights at one end until the whole thing lay flat on the drawing. Finally, centres were marked out at 83 mm and a horizontal at 14 mm from the top of the lower deck windows. U-shaped pieces of strip were soldered to form the support for the bogie bolsters. This was my second mistake. I had not allowed for the difference in thickness of the cast side and the new side. The bogie bolster did not reach across the tram body. So should have made the U shapes from 3 mm wide material rather than 1 mm.

Now the side was removed from the drawing and at last I could see the proper side. Both the new parts were made in one evening while watching television and that included cutting the side pieces from the sheet. The final additions using pre-cut plastic strip, were the bottom horizontal below the doors and the vertical between the two doors on each side. I also had to add the little pieces to form the curves previously mentioned. Normally I would have built the lower saloon keeping the ends separate until after painting and glazing as I did with the Goddess. However, I felt that the joint between the sides and the ends was critical, any misalignment would have been very noticeable. In view of the new side being so much thinner than the old, I decided to fix the ends on before painting to allow a good fit to be made. The end castings were modified by removing the warning light next to the headlight and smoothing the dash. A new warning light was made by wrapping 30-amp fuse wire around a fine rod and cutting it to form a circle. This was glued into place above the headlight. The destination and route number boxes were filled in. Each side was bent slightly at the inner edge of the outer lower deck windows to form the taper towards the ends. The ends and sides were fitted over two evenings using Milliput. This is an epoxy compound in which a blue strip and white strip of putty-like material are mixed together. When left overnight they set into a firm material which has powerful gluing capacity and is easily filed and smoothed.

First each side was fitted to an end, using the Milliput on the inside and leaving it upside down to set. The next day the two sub-assemblies were joined to form the whole body. Then any gaps which were apparent were filled and the joint smoothed down. Care was taken over this in order to remove any irregularity which would have been high-lighted by the painting.

Having satisfied myself with the smoothing down, the painting was started by giving the body, inside and outside, two coats of matt white followed by two of gloss ivory (Humbrol No 41). At the same time the underside of the roof casting was painted white (finishing with gloss) and the screens which were to be placed behind the driver's compartment were given a tan finish (Humbrol Matt No 62). The outside of the body was then masked with tape ready for the red paint. Where the paint followed the curve of the window ends the tape was cut to shape first on the metal sheet reserved for this task. To form the curve the craft knife was run around a small curve of the correct diameter. Any disc or household object of the right size will do. When applied to the tram the curved part was positioned first then the rest laid on. It took a few tries on each strip before I got them into the correct position. As usual, all the tape edges were well

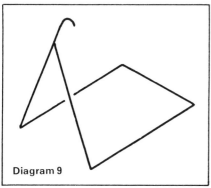

Diagram 9

Above *A Bec E/E1 kit given a simple conversion to an open-top car with reversed stairs. This type of car was used on many systems and this modification opens up many opportunities. For example, the addition of vertical bars in the end windows would give a model of the LCC Classes A and D* (model M. Till, photo D. Voice).

Left Diagram 9: *New trolley hook for No 331, made from nickel silver wire.*

pressed down with a wooden cocktail stick. The two coats of matt red were followed by a coat of gloss. According to the text books the shade of red used on this particular vehicle was noticeably darker than the usual red. So I started with gloss Humbrol No 19 and added a few drops of gloss black, stirring well all the time until it became a darker shade but before becoming a different colour. This was used over the matt red. The centre entrance doors were left until after the masking tape was removed and the red paint had hardened. Then the small errors and unwanted paint flows were touched out. In many instances where excess red had crept over the ivory the red was scraped off carefully to leave the lighter colour underneath. This reduced the possibility of extra lines of paint showing where the touching up had been done. At this stage the lettering and numbers were added. The black lining was drawn in using a drafting pen and Indian ink. The upper and lower edges of the thick black band along the skirt were drawn in using the pen and the rest filled in using a small paint brush. When all was dry the whole body was varnished.

The main roof and cab roofs were painted light grey (mixed from black and white) as were the trolley planks. These were then fitted and holes drilled out for the small tubing forming the trolley fittings which were glued into place. The lower deck, including cabs, were glazed and the interior of the cabs fitted out according to the instructions with the driver being glued on to the seat on the screen forming the rear of the cab. This screen was filed to fit between the Milliput joints. The edges had to coincide with the appropriate window pillars. The upper deck floor was cut from plastic card. The stairwell was cut out and small pieces of plastic card used to represent the protecting barriers around the stairs. The seating, glazing and interior details were all completed in the usual way. Trolley poles were made as described in the previous chapter, ready to be fitted. The roof was made ready to fit by preparing the trolley hooks. Rather than use the white metal castings in the kit, which I felt were too delicate for the usual knocks my models get, I made new hooks from nickel silver wire as in Diagram 9. These were glued, using epoxy resin, to the underside of the roof and the top of the cast ends were filed as needed to allow the roof to fit snugly all around. The roof was then glued into place.

As mentioned before, the sides were too far apart for the bogie support bolsters. To compensate for this I fixed some strip nickel silver to the locating lugs on the bolsters using low-melt solder to enable them to reach the locating points each side of the body. The tops of the bogie bolsters were painted dark grey and they were fitted into place using epoxy resin. One of the prominent internal features of No 331 is the position of the staircases. These were entirely straight and since those provided in the kit have a 90-degree turn, two new staircases were made. The ones in the kit were used as a guide and the sides were cut from plastic card with the stair part from $\frac{3}{16}$ in balsa wood. As it is not easy to see the actual steps I saved time by not cutting them but used the smooth wood and ended up with a slide rather than a staircase. The sides were painted blue (Humbrol Gloss No 14) and the upper and lower surface of the steps dark grey. They were glued into place using the photos to give the correct position. I made sure that there was sufficient clearance for the bogies when fitted. When the stairs were in place it was not possible to see that I had missed out the steps.

The next problem was to hide the bogie power units and avoid the ground being seen through the lower deck windows. This was solved by using some thin card cut to the width of the inside of the tram. A piece was bent and cut to fit from the inner edge of one bogie bolster along the lower edge of the windows to the stairs. It was bent to follow the sloping under-surface of the stairs to the stair bottom, then bent the opposite way to the next set of stairs. Then up the under-surface to the lower edge of the windows and so on to the inner edge of the next bolster. This totally enclosed the area between the two bolsters, did not interfere with the bogies themselves and also allowed the central well to be formed. When I was satisfied with the fit, the card was removed and painted dark grey. The conductor and some passengers were fitted. Full standing passengers could be placed in the central well with the conductor, while head and shoulders represented seated people beyond the stairs. Note that all the lower deck seating was longitudinal, rather reminiscent of some underground railway seating. The two ends beyond the bogie bolsters were also filled with grey painted card cut to size and fitted just below the window level, from the edge of the bolster to the screen at the back of the cab. Again these were fitted with passengers. All the card parts were glued carefully into place. A lump of Blu-Tac on the end of a stick helped to position the small end places.

The fenders, lifeguards and trays were all painted black and glued in the appropriate places on the body. The bogie side frames were purchased from the

Believe it or not this model started life as a Bec E kit. It is now Blackpool works car No 753 on the Bispham to Little Bispham layout of Alan Kirkman. It does show how versatile these kits can be with a little bit of imagination (model A. Kirkman, photo D. Voice).

range of Anbrico spares (part No T5). These have lugs on the back for fixing purposes which are too large for the Bec bogies. I cut them back to the depth of the slot, filed the new edge smooth, then cut a new slot with a hacksaw to fit over the spigot on the bogie. They were fixed on using low-melt solder. The centres of the wheels on the bogie did not quite coincide with the smaller wheel base of the side frame casting, but this was not noticeable when all was fitted together.

The side frames, bogie ends and all lifeguards were painted gloss black. The lifeguards and smaller side guards were fitted under the cab floor with epoxy resin. A piece of balsa wood was used to make a false floor between the cab end and the bogie. This was used to support the life tray. Care was taken not to restrict the swing of the bogie. The final job was to connect the insulated side brushes on the bogies using very flexible insulated wire. It was made long enough to pass under the well of the centre but not too long so as to interfere with the movement of the bogies or drag on to the ground. The bogies were given a last check and light oiling and then No 331 had its final proving run. All went well and it joined the fleet to become one of my favourite models.

The technique of modifying and building tram bodies using metal strips which has been described in this chapter, and will be met again in Chapter Seven, was developed by David Orchard. He has carried out much experimental construction in order to refine the method and iron out the snags. David has generously shared his skills with me and I am grateful to him for readily agreeing to my describing his methods in this book. I consider it to be a major contribution to tramway modelling and I can vouch for the ease and speed of construction.

Chapter 6

Research, painting and lining

Research

When modelling a particular prototype tram it is satisfying to know that everything is right about the finished model. This means that you must be aware of the principal features of the original tram and to achieve this some form of research is necessary. The most complete and enjoyable way is to visit the real thing, if it still exists. Indeed, I would recommend that every tram modeller should try to see, and ride on, one of the many trams running in this country. Even if an example of your particular tram does not exist, the atmosphere of the real thing can only do your model good. Many of the awkward questions on detail can be resolved by looking at similar types of vehicle. In Appendix Three there is a list of those places where trams can be seen and, in some cases, ridden. For the modeller the best place is surely the National Tramway Museum at Crich with its large numbers of trams from many different systems. Have a good look around, particularly at the details not often found in photos. For example the layout of the driving position, the various types of seating arrangements, the colours of the floors, ceilings and interior sides. I could go

The sort of detail shot invaluable to the modeller. This shows the maximum traction bogie on Bolton 66. It also emphasises the superb job of restoration the enthusiasts have done in rebuilding and preserving this tram (photo D. Voice).

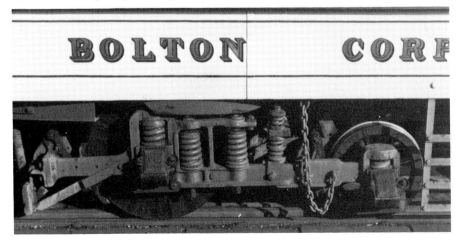

on. If you are modelling one of the preserved cars take lots of photographs, if permitted, from as many angles as you can easily obtain. If possible, include a shot or two of the roof. This is not always an easy photograph to take but one which proves invaluable. The coloured postcards which may be available are also useful so do not miss out on them.

Although we are lucky to have so many preserved trams in this country, they only represent a very small proportion of the actual numbers and types which did run in our towns. So it is quite likely that your particular prototype does not exist any more, or perhaps it is out of easy reach of you. In this case a different approach needs to be taken. So let me assume that, to start with, you had nothing but an idea of the vehicle which you would like to model and that there are no kits for your particular tram. You are probably wondering where to start. My first advice would be to join one or more of the tramway societies. I am biased, of course, to the Tramway and Light Railway Society but the Tramway Museum Society is also useful. Both groups have photographic sales covering many of the systems in this country. The third national tramway society is the Light Rail Transit Association which has an historic interest through its particular publication *Tramway Review*. Most of these photographs are reproductions of very early pictures and are, by necessity, black and white. You may find a few different views of the type of car which you are after. Also other members in the societies may be able to help if you get really stuck. There are regular magazines sent out by all groups to their members and a request published in one would be sure to result in information.

The next line of enquiry would be to see if there is a book covering the system or that part of the country where the system ran. If such a book is still in print it would be possible to obtain it from the many booksellers specialising in tramway books and some are listed in Appendix Four while others can be found in the advertisements of the magazine *Modern Tramway* (a monthly published jointly by Ian Allan and the Light Rail Transit Association). A trip to your library could be useful, although my experience is that the number of tram books kept on the shelves is somewhat limited. However, it is worth while to try two sections, the Dewey Decimal main numbers 388 and 625. If the system you are after happens to be your own home town then do not forget to ask at the library. They will often have local interest books in a reference section and may even have photos of the tramway on special files that may require the librarian's permission to gain access.

The ease of this research depends rather on how long ago the prototype ran and whether someone else has done the research for you by publishing a book. For the very early trams, there are articles to be found in the professional journals of the day. Those which I have come across include *Tramway and Railway World, Lightning, The Electrical Engineer* and *The Electrical Review*. Again check with the main reference library near you to see if they are kept. When I was considering constructing one of the original single-deck tramcar and trailer sets which ran on the Kidderminster and Stourport Tramway, I did this sort of research. Luckily, I am able to get to the magnificent reference library in Birmingham and, knowing the date that the line opened, I went through the appropriate volumes. Sure enough, each did contain an illustrated article on the system including photos of the trams and details of their overall measurements. The library did not have the early copies of the *Tramway and Railway World*. So I put in a request indicating the article I wanted and the

Above *The roof of a Blackpool Standard car at Crich (on a busy day!). This is the view most people get of models but is rarely seen on the real thing.*

Right *Longitudinal seating. This is Dudley and Stourbridge No 5, a single-deck car built without bulkheads and restored by enthusiasts to run at the Black Country Museum* (photo D. Voice).

Left *Transverse seating on the top deck of a Blackpool Standard car at Crich. This is very typical of the seating on pre-war trams* (photo D. Voice).

Below *Detail of the controller, set to the left of the driving position. The handbrake is just visible on the right in this view of Dudley and Stourbridge No 5* (photo D. Voice).

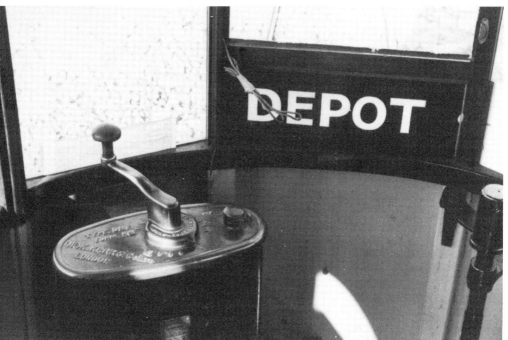

date. A few weeks later a photocopy of the relevant pages arrived at my home and, to my delight, included a small drawing of the vehicles. Although when comparing these with the photos I knew that they could not be relied upon for accuracy. With all this information, backed up by the very comprehensive description of the system and fleet in *Black Country Trams, Volume 2* written and published by Stan Webb, developing the drawings for the model was quite easy. With those systems which ran during the post-war period the amount of information which is available is naturally more prolific and this is illustrated in the later chapter on constructing the Mumbles car.

The task can be made easier if a good drawing of the vehicle can be found. However, it is necessary to put in a word of warning here. Please do not think that because a drawing exists that it must be accurate. All drawings should be thoroughly checked. First the accuracy of the drawing should be checked against the scale measurements. Often the draughtsman will make a mistake in measurement and the drawing, while looking reasonable, may be too long, too high or too wide. Also the window spacing should be carefully examined as this is where all kinds of errors creep into the drawing. Next the drawing should be compared with a photo of the car to make sure that there are no differences. Often tramcars went through a number of re-builds in their lifetime, as well as the usual repairs. This was particularly the case where there had been extensive accident damage at any time. The result was often that a batch of cars, which were identical when new, may have had a lot of differences in detail near the end of their running life. When I was researching the Mumbles car I soon realised that while the 13 trams looked identical at first glance each had its own identifying features different from the other 12. To overcome this problem I usually pick one of the photographs which I have that shows the tram in the appropriate style of livery and use that as the master from which I work, including, of course, the number of the vehicle. I then use the other photos to pick up detail which cannot be seen or worked out from the master photo. Even then some parts have to be guessed at, although this is less of a problem as experience with tram design grows. The usual problem is seat layouts, particularly on open-top cars. I hope that the early chapters can help you with that difficulty.

Painting

I mentioned choosing an appropriate style of livery. I feel this is important as the visual impact of the model depends very much on its colour and style of paintwork. A good indicator of how difficult and how much time will be spent on the paintwork is to count the number of colour changes from bottom to top. Note that I am not referring to the number of colours but the number of times one colour finishes and another starts. A tram with five colour changes, such as the Mumbles car described in the next chapter, is quite easy. If you are thinking of making a model with colour changes which go into double figures be prepared for a long job. There is another problem with liveries and that is determining the proper colours to use. Often the modeller is confronted with a range of black and white postcards and perhaps a printed description. Now trying to determine the correct shade from a printed description, especially if it is the 'official' one issued by the management of the tramway, is a thankless task.

I am reminded of the story of tramway researchers who were trying to determine the exact colour of a long closed system. After many years of searching they traced the actual man who had the job of re-painting the cars during the winter months. They first asked where the paint had come from, hoping to find the manufacturer. The old man replied that he always went down the road to the local paint shop. Not deterred they asked what colour he used. Back came the answer 'Green'. 'What shade of green?'. 'Well', said the old man, 'I always asked for a pretty green.' I use this example to explain why I never get too worried about colour for my models. Naturally, the best is to see the actual colour and this is sometimes possible by visiting a preserved tramcar. The range of preserved liveries is quite extensive and a great help to the modeller. Colour photographs and postcards are also useful. However, care must be taken with some of these reproductions as the colour is not always true.

Check out the background details in order to determine the accuracy of colour. Also drawings and paintings may help although the artists can and do make errors over this aspect of their work.

When it comes down to it the modeller will often have to mix up a colour as near as he can determine. Again I do not worry too much about exact shades as the actual trams often varied considerably in colour depending on how long they had been on the road since their last re-paint. This effect can easily be seen today on bus fleets. The colour changes noticeably as the paint ages. Also one would expect that today's paints would be consistent in colour from batch to batch. But my own observations show this is not the case and even when freshly painted the vehicles can vary in colour. I am sure that this was even more apparent in the days when the tram companies often mixed their own paints or did, as the old man related, buy off the shelf whatever was available.

Another aspect of colour is finding out which particular parts of the tram were painted which colours. Here a combination of black and white photos and your own experience can help a great deal. It is possible, by careful examination, to have a fair idea of the changes in colour from the black and white photos, although there are many traps for the unwary. But on the credit side the basic style of livery was very similar for the older type of tram. The underfloor details and trucks were usually painted red oxide, later black was introduced and became more accepted after the mid-'30s. The lower saloon would have the lighter colour on the window frames and the lower rocker panel while the upper rocker panel and dash would be in the darker colour. The inside of the dash was usually red oxide (it is safe to use this if no further information becomes available). The stairs would have the darker colour on the sides with the lighter colour underneath. Treads would be dark grey while the risers were often of the lighter colour. On open-top cars the decency panels were usually the light colour with a line of dark colour separating the upper and lower decks. The inside of the decency panel is more of a problem as there seemed to be a choice of red oxide, black or the light colour from the livery. On balcony and enclosed cars the light colour was used on the window framing while the dark colour may or may not have been applied to the side panels and upper dash. There were variations to this. Two words of warning, when a photo shows the light striking the side of a tram in a three-quarter view sometimes the dark colour will appear light and lining out is made invisible. This is why I have put so much emphasis on getting as many photos as possible.

Having gathered all the information and used it in the construction of the tram, the major influence on the quality of your model will then be the way that you paint it. I am sure that you, like me, have seen superb models complete to the smallest detail look awful because of poor painting. Indeed such is the importance that I place on painting that I spend probably three times as long painting as actually constructing the model. There is no doubt that a mediocre model can be turned into a prize winner by careful painting, while poor painting will reduce the value of any model. My own preference is to brush paint rather than use the new airbrush sprays. I have seen examples of models painted with the airbrushes and they can produce absolutely superb finishes in a very short time. However, with the more elaborate type of tram livery it would still be necessary to spend time on brush painting. For this reason I have never got myself an airbrush but have always relied on the tried and tested methods of painting.

Above *A streamline bogie car with the final coat of Liverpool green paint drying and waiting for the masking strips of self-adhesive tape to be removed* (photo D. Voice).

Right *Peeling the tape carefully away to reveal the desired sharp line between the green and white paint. So far no touching up is necessary* (photo D. Voice).

Below *Using a fine (00) brush to paint out the unwanted areas of dark paint that crept under the masking. Compare this with the finished model in Chapter 3* (photo D. Voice).

The first requirement is to have suitable brushes. To begin with I recommend a No 4 and a No 00. As modelling experience grows so the range can be expanded until a full set from No 00 to No 5 is obtained. This will give you the chance to discover exactly the size which is most comfortable for you to use for various jobs. Naturally, when starting with just two brushes the larger is used for most of the painting and the smaller for picking out details and touching up. Now all the best books on painting insist on using sable brushes. I must agree that they are the best but are also very expensive. I have been able to get equal results from good quality hair brushes at about half the price. Nylon brushes, in my experience, are not so good. The cheap ones are terrible and the expensive ones not as good as an equally priced natural hair brush. Having got the brushes the next item is the paint. There are a number of manufacturers specialising in paint for modellers and again it is very much personal preference as to which you choose. I have always been satisfied with the Humbrol range and so have tended to use them predominantly. In the previous chapters you will have seen reference to matt and gloss paints. Whenever possible, I use matt paint and produce the required gloss finish by varnishing afterwards. Matt paint has a number of advantages over gloss. It dries quicker; it seems to have a more opaque texture and so covers better; and it is possible to apply further coats to small parts of a larger area without the addition being noticeable. On this last point is is not possible to add a little touching up to gloss paint as it always stands out like a sore thumb. Where it is needed the whole panel has to be re-painted.

Paint is a thin layer of colour applied to the model. So, whatever the surface of the model is like, the paint will show it. Therefore, it is important to ensure that the surface before painting is as perfect as possible. All smears of excess glue must be cleaned off and any rough surfaces smoothed down with fine wet-and-dry paper (the same as is sold in car do-it-yourself shops for rubbing down the bodies of motor cars when re-painting). On cast items of kits all the flash should have been removed before assembly, but it is worth checking again. All joints and any other unwanted gaps should be filled. I use the plastic putty used by modellers for drastic alterations to plastic kits, although I have also seen good reports on the use of Milliput. The gaps should be filled proud of the surface and, when set, smoothed down with files and wet-and-dry paper. In this way the joints can be completely concealed. When you are satisfied the first coat of paint can be applied. In the case of brass models this should be etching primer, in order to reduce to a minimum the risk of paint chipping off at a later date. I have had difficulty in obtaining this primer but my experience shows that it is worth the effort, even if you have to order by post. This self-etching primer can be used on other metals, but they are not as crucial as brass. It should never be used on plastic and is not needed on white metal which seems to soak up the paint a little like a sponge. This helps to form an excellent key for the paint. Where self-etching primer is not used the first few coats should be of matt paint even if the required colour is only available in gloss. In such cases the nearest colour in the matt range should be used as an undercoat. Where the desired colour is available in matt then it should be used straight away. In all cases new pots of paint should be purchased for each model. Old paint gets bits in it that can ruin a model in just a single coat.

My preference is to put on the lightest colour first, usually painting the tram inside and out. With the older type of car I usually finish the interior in dark brown. After the first coat the body is inspected as faults or rough surfaces missed during the preparation of the body will now be highlighted. These should be rubbed down before putting any more paint on the model. After a few more coats (leaving at least overnight for each coat to dry off thoroughly before applying the next) the colour should have an even depth all over. With matt colours three coats are usually sufficient, although do not hesitate to add more if you are in any doubts about the finished colour. The livery will now need darker colours to be added. Apart from the smooth finish, or lack of it, the next most important aspect of painting is to achieve really clean boundary lines between one colour and another. In this respect the model must be more accurate than the real thing. If you closely inspect the line between colour changes on most public service vehicles, you will see that it has been done by hand and often is distinctly uneven. However, the eye, at the normal viewing distance ignores this unevenness and sees a clean line. On a model any blemish on the same line seems to be highlighted and the eye can hardly draw itself away from what is a very small error. So the modeller needs to get as close to perfection as possible. However, if your hands are like mine, any attempt to do it free-hand would lead to total disaster. Therefore, some extra help is required and luckily can be found in the common clear self-adhesive tape. This I use as a masking tape to ensure a clean division between the colours. There are a few precautions which are needed. Do not use the existing edge of the tape as it seems to collect dust and gets somewhat ragged. It is better to lay the required length on some clean scrap metal (I keep a special sheet of tin plate just for this and lining out tape) and with a clean new blade in the craft knife cut a new edge. I peel off the tape and stick it on to the model over the paint which is to be protected and to form the edge in the required place. If you miss the right place first time you can carefully peel off the tape and try again. It is best not to rip off the tape quickly as this may remove some of the paint from the model. If this does happen then repaint the affected area before beginning the masking off again.

When you are happy that it is in the right place press the edge down hard using a wooden cocktail stick. The tape will actually change colour slightly when pressed down so make sure that this happens the full length of the edge (this is to prevent the next coats of paint seeping under the tape). Use special care at any corners or projections on the model. No matter how careful you are, internal corners are awkward and about half tend to allow some seepage. The darker colour is applied allowing an overlap on to the tape and making sure that the edge is completely covered in paint. Sufficient coats are applied to get the depth and consistency of colour required. About two to three hours after the last coat has been applied the tape is removed. This is important as the paint should still be reasonably plastic although fairly dry. If it is allowed to harden completely it tends to shatter along the edge as the tape is removed giving an unwanted uneven edge. As the paint is still hardening, care should be taken to avoid touching it. To remove the tape, do not rip it off as some of the lighter colour paint will probably be pulled off as well. The least damage is done by folding it back on itself and then pulling gently while checking the tape as it comes off the model. If any light paint does start to come away stop and try taking the tape from the other end until it is removed completely. There will still be a need to rectify the damage but provided care is taken the chances of doing such damage are remote.

However, there will probably be a need to touch up the edge after the tape is removed. This is where the matt paint is such an advantage. Using the smaller sizes of brushes the offending parts can be over-painted. As this usually occurs on internal corners it is quite a straight-forward job. If you had to use gloss paint as the first colour this type of touching-up would probably not be practical. The alternative in such cases is to scrape away the unwanted dark colour very carefully to leave the light colour underneath showing. The gloss surface actually helps as it provides less grip for the extra paint. When doing this job first run a new blade along the colour boundary to sever the unwanted excess away from the paint that is in the correct place. There is then less danger of removing the wrong part of the paint. The finish using this technique is so good that I use it for nearly all parts of the tram where there is a change of colour. The few exceptions are parts that can be painted separately before fixing on the tram, and where only relatively small areas of colour meet, such as truck sides, headlights and stair treads.

Lining

Once the major colours have been applied the problem of lining can be tackled. There are a variety of techniques available and I find that it is best to be able to put your hand to two or three, using the most suitable for the particular task. With wide bands going around the body, such as colour bands around the upper and lower edges of the top deck of many open-top liveries, or the thin bands around the later Sheffield livery, the masking technique described above is highly satisfactory. In the case of wide bands that are panelled, such as the brown and cream livery of early LCC cars, a draughting pen can be used. This type of pen can be adjusted to width and should be loaded using a small paint brush. Ideally Indian ink is most suitable but may not be available in the colour required. Therefore, the appropriate paint should be used but thinned down until it runs easily off the pen. If using this type of pen is new to you it is best to have a good practice on paper until you feel confident. My own technique is to load the pen just before using it (and after each line wiping the pen perfectly clean again with a piece of tissue). Then the line is drawn as required using either a straight edge or a raised edge on the model if there is a convenient one (often kits have raised edges representing lining). At the start there will be a slight blob but this can be reduced by moving the pen along the edge just before touching it to the model. Try to keep each line continuous as any break in the drawing will tend to show. The line is kept as thin as is comfortable to draw and where wider lines are required two lines should be drawn at the required distance and the gap filled with paint using a small brush. In the case of kit-built LCC cars the raised edge moulded in the side is used as a guide both for the pen and the other edge of the colour when filled in with the small brush.

The final technique is used for the fine lining such as the gold lines around the dash and rocker panels. Here I used the metallic type of self-adhesive tape which can be found in stationers particularly at Christmas time. A length should be laid on a clean metal surface and it should be an inch or so longer than the panel to be lined. Using a new point on the blade of the craft knife and a metal rule, cut the tape into very thin strips. It is impossible to measure them so do it by eye and cut three or four times as many as you will need. Using tweezers raise each strip in turn being sure to hold both ends before it leaves the surface. Failure to do this will result in a curled up strip only good for the waste bin. Lay the strips

The technique of lining out with tape has been used to create the panelling effect on this model of a Liverpool car of the 758-769 series (model and photo D. Orchard).

on a clear part of the metal surface. They will vary in width so choose sufficient of the required width.

Place the strip on the tram. If you miss the right place, gently raise it again and keep trying until all is well. Minor adjustments are made with a cocktail stick. Using the same stick, press carefully the full length making sure the strip is stuck properly. Leave the excess on and continue with the other strips, taking care not to disturb any lining previously laid. Make sure there is excess on every strip. Leave it 24 hours to let the stretch in the strips shrink back. Cut the strips to length using a sharp curved blade, I keep a new one for this job alone to ensure a good edge. The blade is lightly pressed on the strip to cut it.

If the lining is not gold or silver, one of the other metallic colours could be used, but they do look a little odd. A better solution is to use ordinary PVC coloured tape. This is very much thicker than the metallic tape but from normal viewing distance this is not too noticeable. The same method is used as described before except the tape should be left for 48 hours before trimming because the PVC stretches greatly. When the lining is complete it should be fixed in place using clear varnish. Use a fresh tin of varnish for each model to ensure a glass smooth surface. Provided the model is handled normally, there is no fear that the lining will come adrift even under heavy use such as exhibition work. This technique is also a useful way to add beading and similar fine detail to models. In this case the thickness of the PVC tape is an advantage and, since it will be painted, the original colour of the tape is irrelevant.

The last touches to add to the model are numbers, company name, destination blinds, route numbers and advertisements. There is a wide range of all types available as water slide transfers from Mabex (see Appendix Four). Other types of water slide transfers are available with letters, numbers and ornate scroll work. In all of these types I find it best to trim them as close to the pattern as possible before applying them. After soaking for a few minutes the backing paper can be slid off and the transfer applied. If a small blob of water is put on the model before the transfer it allows it to be moved around until in the correct place. The transfer should then be pressed with a clean cloth and left overnight to dry before giving the complete panel a coat of varnish. The other

type of transfer that is useful for models is the dry print. Here the number or letter is positioned then rubbed on to the model through the holding sheet. A sheet of small numbers and letters suitable for OO gauge models is produced by Blick and a variety of colours is available.

For complex fleet names, special advertisements or particular crests it is possible to make your own water slide transfer. Some white gummed paper should be fixed to a board with the gummed side uppermost. It should be given three coats of varnish and then the required name or crest can be painted or applied using transfers to get the desired result. This is fixed into place with a further coat of varnish. The transfer is cut out and soaked off the backing paper in the usual way. When removed from the backing paper the homemade transfer should be handled with great care as it is very much more fragile than its commercially made counterpart.

When the model is complete it should be kept in a protected place which for me means a specially made or adapted box. I have now standardised on a box 9½ × 4 × 1½ in made from corrugated cardboard taken from boxes obtained gratis from super-markets. I use them inside out so that any printing or advertising is relegated to the inside. Once made, the inside of the box is tailored to fit the tram snugly using strips of corrugated cardboard. The strips are bent and glued into position to allow the model to fit perfectly. It is an advantage to have removable trolley poles which are stored in a compartment next to the model. However, it is possible to adapt the box to take a model with non-removable trolley poles. Naturally, there has to be a separate box for each model that you have. I label each one on the end and stack them side by side so that in storage the tram is standing upright in the box. The collection tends to look like a row of books on the shelf. I only take my trams out when actually working on them, running them on the layout or showing them to other people. This does not mean that I am not able easily to view the whole collection and I cannot say that the boxes enhance the room like the finished models would. However, having spent so much time in making a model I do like to ensure that they are kept in as good a condition as possible and this way does mean that they are kept free from dust and the little fingers of the younger members of the family. I also use the boxes for transporting the models to and from exhibitons and so on. They have saved many a model from a lengthy repair job. On the worst occasion I dropped one down a full flight of stairs. It was horrifying to watch the box, knowing there was a tram inside, gracefully bouncing down. Each bounce getting bigger than the last until, with a nasty thud, it came to rest at the bottom. When I opened the box the packing strips were bent out of recognition. But the damage to the model was repaired in an evening and I did not have to rebuild the model as I had feared.

Top left *The home-made transfer for the Croydon Corporation Tramways name on the rocker panel. The coat of arms is from the Mabex range of model vehicle transfers. Lining out is with metallic self-adhesive tape as described in the text* (model and photo D. Voice).

Left *Having spent hours perfecting your model it is worthwhile spending a few minutes to make a custom-built protection and carrying box. This shows the horse tram safely in its box* (model and photo D. Voice).

Left *These models of LCC trams use every technique described in the text. When finished they are really eye-catching, all well worth the work involved* (models and photo D. Voice).

Chapter 7

Scratch-building

When deciding to scratch-build a tram there is no limit on the subject. Unlike kits, where the choice is up to the preference of the kit manufacturer, the scratch-builder has full freedom. In choosing a tram to model in this chapter I could have chosen any tram of any system. Indeed the choice was embarrassingly large. In the end my decision was to build one of the most distinctive cars to run in this country. The Swansea and Mumbles tramcar is instantly recognisable and even people who are not interested in trams know this car. It is also claimed to be the largest tram ever run in the country, although the new Jubilee Class being built in Blackpool must be another contender for this title.

Before entering into the construction of the model, it is worthwhile discovering a little of the history of these trams and the lines on which they ran. The Swansea and Mumbles Railway holds the honour of being the first line in the world to carry a regular passenger service, albeit horse-drawn. The line was opened in 1806 and was very much a tram road having angle-iron spiked to granite blocks, the wheels of the trucks being flangeless. The line was all laid as reserved track, where it ran by roads the track was laid to the side of, rather than in, the roadway. The passenger service began in 1807 and by 1860 was running with open-top double-deck cars pulled by a single horse. Access to the upper deck was by steps either end of the car but both steps were on the same side, so even from the earliest days passengers only boarded from the landward side of the line. The angle-iron was replaced by flat bottomed railway rail from 1855 to 1860 and the gauge of the track was changed from 4 ft to 4 ft 8½ in. In 1877 steam power was introduced to the line and up until 1896 there was a mixture of steam and horse-drawn traffic. After that year the horses disappeared. The line still went under the title of a railway and the locomotives were very much railway rather than tramway in design. However, the passenger cars continued to have their tram features in being double-deck open-top trailers with spiral stairs at the ends. The 0-6-0 and 0-4-0 side and saddle tank locomotives were obviously very powerful by tram standards. Photos exist of trains consisting of up to 20 double-deck trailers all packed to over-flowing with passengers (as many as 1,000 on the one train) hauled by one locomotive.

In 1929 the new electric cars began operation and this service lasted until 1960 when the last public tram left Rutland Street at 10.05 am to be followed at 11.42 am by a pair of decorated cars carrying the official party to declare the line closed. There were 13 electric cars each capable of seating 106 passengers.

Top *Two Mumbles trams in a typical 'train'. This shows the seaward side, without entrances. Note also the panelled and painted windows hiding the stairs* (photo The Mumbles Railway Company Limited).

Above *Tram No 1, the one I chose to model, heads this 'train'. This is a view of the landward side, with the entrances. The detail on the front of the tram is clearly shown* (photo The Mumbles Railway Company Limited).

Eleven were built to open the newly electrified line in 1929 and in 1930 a further two were added. Following on the tradition of boarding from the landward side only, the entrances were both on the same side of the car. The power was picked up from the overhead wire by a pantograph set over the centre of one of the bogies. The pantograph was a most unusual tram feature at the time the cars

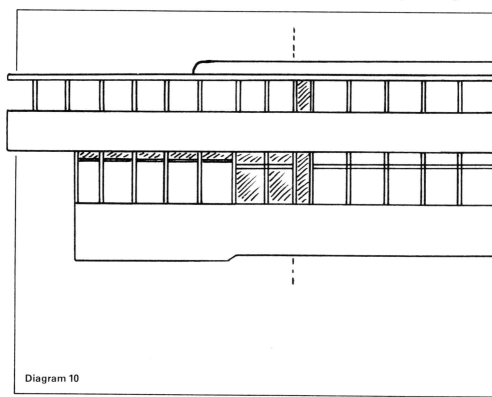

Diagram 10

Diagram 10: *Negative drawing for constructing Swansea and Mumbles Tramcar. One side to be made to full drawing and one side between dotted lines only.*

were built. Jumper leads were fitted to allow the trams to be coupled in pairs and driven from the front cab. These pairs were referred to by the local population as 'trains' and, indeed, they ran on railway type track. There was never any grooved rail or street running as would be found on most tramway systems. However, nearly all authorities are agreed that these electric vehicles were very much trams rather than railway coaches.

In 1960 one of these large trams, No 2, was bought for preservation by the Middleton Railway Preservation Society. Unfortunately, the only storage available was unprotected and a combination of vandalism and weather deterioration led to the car being broken up. The only reminder which exists is the end of car No 7, saved by the Railway Club of Wales and held in storage prior to exhibition in one of the museums in Swansea.

In the previous chapter I have referred to the importance of research when building models. This is absolutely necessary when scratch-building because, of course, you are beginning with a clean sheet. There are no kit parts to start you off. So the first task is to gather information, drawings and photos of the Mumbles car. As this formed part of one of the later systems to close down, there is quite a lot of information readily available. The history of the line with photos and information on the electric cars can be found in *The Swansea and Mumbles Railway* by Charles E. Lee, published by The Oakwood Press. When

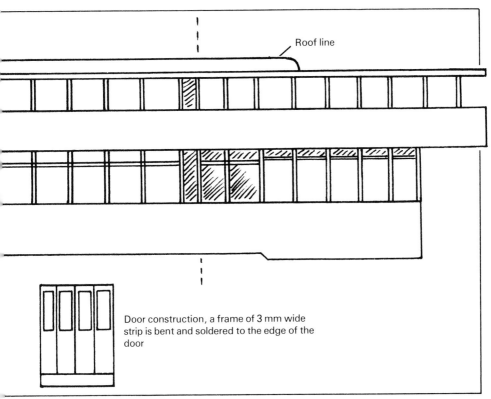

Door construction, a frame of 3 mm wide strip is bent and soldered to the edge of the door

it came to a drawing of the tram there was one complication, I was not able to find a 4 mm scale diagram. However, an excellent drawing in 7 mm (O gauge) can be purchased for a modest sum from Terry Russell. (I have since discovered that a blueprint was produced by Skinley as part of their range of 4 mm drawings.) A large selection of postcards (mostly black and white but including two colour ones) is available from the Mumbles Railway Company. Their address and that of Terry Russell can be found in Appendix Four. Another coloured picture can be found in *Trams in Colour Since 1945* by J. Joyce, published by the Blandford Press. Black and white pictures are included in most of the British tram picture collections which have recently been published. Armed with all this material a confident start can be made.

From the O gauge drawing, or 4 mm blueprint, a working negative can be drawn. Actually, in the case of the Mumbles car, there is no difference between positive and negative so a straight drawing is started. A pocket calculator is very useful at this stage if the dimensions are taken off the O gauge drawing, since each measurement has to be multiplied by four and divided by seven to get the correct OO gauge size. In my usual way I drew the horizontals first to define the top and bottom of each side and the correct spacing for the upper and lower limits of the windows. Then the vertical window pillars were drawn in the correct place. I kept checking the drawing against the photographs to make sure that the proportion looked correct. This part of the drawing was purely of the side and did not include the entrances. The ends were drawn to these sides by unwrapping them. This meant getting the true lengths of the dash and vestibule parts and these were taken from the plan view. I used the very simple method of following the curved lines with a piece of cotton then measuring the cotton. A full size drawing of my negative is shown in Diagram 10.

I had chosen to place the joints above the inner edge of each entrance. In the normal type of tram this would have meant making two sides exactly the same then joining them after shaping the curves on the ends. But the Mumbles car has both entrances on the same side, so the construction is a little different. Both ends were made up on one side using the whole of Diagram 10, while the second side was much shorter and only extended between the dotted lines. For this part of the construction a separate drawing was used for each side as the heat of the soldering iron tended to burn holes in them.

The sides were made in the same way as described in the construction of the Feltham car No 331 (Chapter Five). However, in the case of the Mumbles car I used brass instead of nickel silver as I found a shop which provided a very good selection of narrow strip, but only in brass. The drawing was taped to some scrap wood and the appropriately sized strips of metal laid into place and soldered together. Although I tried to keep the heat to a minimum during construction by soldering at alternate ends and not letting the soldering iron rest on the metal longer than necessary, the side still twisted slightly. This was corrected by re-touching the necessary joints with the soldering iron until the side lay nice and flat. The length of Code 80 rail was tacked into place to stiffen the side and form the upper-deck floor support. Finally two small pieces of scrap metal were soldered on the shorter of the two sides inside the upper deck panel with half of each piece over-hanging the side. These were to be the fixing plates to solder on to the other side when it was bent to shape. After removing the sides from the drawings, they were washed in hot water with detergent. This was to clean all the flux off.

Then a scale plan was outlined (Diagram 11) and the ends of the longer side carefully bent to form the curve ends. This must be done with care to avoid forming creases. I used a wooden dowel as a former to shape the ends around and checked the curve frequently against the drawing and the made-up second side. When I was satisfied, I soldered the two sides together using the fixing plates. This was done by laying the side to be fixed on the scrap wood and pressing the soldering iron on top of the fixing plate until the tinned area melted and fixed the sides together. Then the upper strips were joined with a touch of solder. This was repeated for the other end. Again the body was washed in hot water and detergent using an old toothbrush to make sure that all the flux had been removed. The body was given a coat of self-etching primer inside and out. This is particularly important on brass to minimise the risk of paint being chipped off. It is also a good idea to use this paint on nickel silver scratch-built trams. One word of warning, make sure that there are no plastic parts as the self-etching primer will not do them any good at all.

The photograph showed clearly that some of the window areas were in fact panelled in. Rather than risk unsoldering parts already in place I decided to use plastic card glued over the window openings. The strip running along the length of the rocker panel was cut from strip plastic card and glued into place. The two doors were constructed in the same manner as the sides, the recess being formed from 3 mm wide brass strip bent to the correct shape and then soldered to the door. The vertical relief where the doors folded was introduced by soldering brass wire in the appropriate places. The completed doors were then glued to the

Above *The assembled body. The joint of the two side assemblies can be seen above the left-hand edge of the entrance. The body has been given a coat of self-etching primer and it is now safe to add the plastic card panelling and plastic strip waist rail* (photo D. Voice).

Right Diagram 11: *Seating and outline plan for Swansea and Mumbles Tramcar.*

Below and bottom *Upper and lower deck detail showing the seat layout. The upper deck photo is a later shot when the drop frame windows had been replaced with a type found on buses. There are alternate fixed glass and sliding vents. I chose to model the earlier windows* (photo The Mumbles Railway Company Limited).

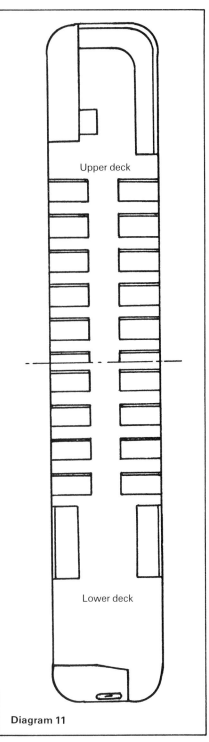

Upper deck

Lower deck

Diagram 11

tram body. When set, I found small gaps between the doors and the frame and these were filled with plastic filler then smoothed off. The body was then carefully examined to check that it was the correct shape and that all the window openings looked right.

The headlamps were added by using some thin-wall 4 mm diameter brass tubing. The end was cut to 45 degrees then a 5 mm length (measured along the longest edge) cut off. Four of these were made. They were then filled with Milliput and stuck in the correct place on the dash. The difference between the curve of the dash and the 45 degree cut of the tube was taken up by the Milliput and any excess was trimmed away before it set. They were left overnight and then a ¼ in drill was run over the end to drill out some of the Milliput and form the dimple of the headlight. The jumper lead sockets were more of a problem until I thought of using nails. 1 in nails were sawn a millimetre from the head and this gave the desired shape. The head was glued to the dash making sure that they were fixed on the entrance side of the car at each end. The upper deck panel was given two coats of matt white and two of gloss white. A strip of self-adhesive tape was cut on some flat metal, as described in the previous chapter, to the width of the white band and then placed in position just below the window level. The edges were pressed down using a cocktail stick.

The distinctive red colour was mixed from Humbrol Matt Red No 60 with a fair bit of Matt Brown Humbrol No 70 until the right shade was reached. I used the coloured photo and postcard as a guide although they did differ in the reproduction. I am not sure even now whether I have got it right but it does have a nice atmosphere. When I showed a friend who remembers travelling on the Mumbles lines he did agree with the colour I had used. The body was given two coats inside and out.

The tape was carefully removed to form the white band and the whole thing was given a coat of varnish. A plastic card floor was cut and one side and painted dark brown. It was then glued into place on the stiffening rails. Acetate sheet was cut to form the glazing and this was trimmed to length by trial and error and glued into place. On the lower deck it can be held in place by being pushed against the recesses of the entrance. The upper deck joints were placed behind two of the panels and the edges of the acetate butted together.

The next part to be made was the chassis. The wheelbase on these bogies was 4 ft 6 in which scaled to 18 mm, a little large for Bec bogies. However, if nothing more suitable can be found the Bec bogies should be used. As it happens I came across a Mehanotehnika articulated chassis which someone had tried to convert into a bogie car and which was rather the worse for the attempt. However, it was very cheap and proved to be ideal, with a slight amount of work, for the Mumbles car. The chassis was sawn across just past the motor to leave the motor, the drive unit and driven bogie as a sub-assembly. The other chassis with the trailing bogie was cut to form a butt joint with the previous part such that the distance betwen the centres of the bogies was 75 mm. A strengthening piece of plastic card was glued above and across the butt joint and the whole thing allowed to set over-night, having first secured everything in place with clothes pegs. The pick-ups on the trailing bogies were connected to the motor. A further set of pick-ups made from strip phosphor bronze (purchased from the model railway shops) were cut to size, soldered to a connecting wire and fitted to the power bogie. They were held in place by a blob of epoxy resin. The connecting wires were soldered to the appropriate brush holder on the motor.

The chassis as rebuilt from a Mehanotehnika Boeing articulated tram. Extra pick-ups were added to the driven bogie to allow all eight wheels to gather current from the track (photo D. Voice).

I could not find side frame castings of the right wheel base so made my own from small pieces of plastic card. These were not as detailed as the usual white metal castings which I buy but, as the usual view of a model tram is from above, I felt there was no serious loss. These side frames were glued into place using the existing mouldings on the bogies as supports. After testing to ensure that all was well, the side frames were painted black using first a matt paint then a gloss. As there was more work to do on the tram body the chassis was put to one side.

The roof was made from ¼ in thick balsa wood cut to the correct length and width to fit the body. The corners were rounded to shape using a sanding block and the edges were curved in the same way. A second piece of balsa was cut from $\frac{1}{32}$ in thick sheet to fit into the upper deck area. It was then glued under the first piece so that the assembly fitted neatly into the body. Then the balsa was coated with sander sealer. I was given a very useful tip some years ago to help get a really superb finish on balsa wood. The sander sealer should have talcum powder (any sort will do) added to it and well stirred in. When smoothed down and painted the finish can be just like metal. So after giving the first coat, the sander sealer was smoothed down with fine sandpaper. I used one of the sponge foam blocks with emery cloth glued to it. The fine side gives a good finish and the foam allows the sanding block to shape to the curved parts. I kept putting coats of sealer on and sanding them down until I thought all the grain marks had been filled and smoothed off. I then gave it a coat of light grey paint. This was mixed by putting a few drops of gloss black into a tin of gloss white. The underside was given a couple of coats of white paint. Finally the roof details near the pantograph were added using plastic card and strip and given another coat of light grey. Careful note was taken to ensure that the pantograph was positioned at the correct end of the car.

Actually, during this part of the construction I made quite a large mistake. Having put a few coats of sander sealer on and smoothed it down I thought that the roof was ready for the light grey paint. However, after giving it a coat I felt that some of the grain was showing through so I decided to apply some more sander sealer. This proved disastrous as the sealer has a cellulose base and it

Above *A test run on the track. The only remaining details to be finished are destination blinds (I was waiting for them to arrive from Mabex) and the addition of longer contacts on the pan of the pantograph* (model and photo D. Voice).

Below *London Transport (ex-LCC) No 1. A fine OO gauge model scratch-built by David Orchard, originator of the method of construction described in the text* (model and photo D. Orchard).

bubbled the enamel paint as effectively as the best paint stripper. So it all had to be removed back to the bare wood and it was a case of starting all over again.

For the pantograph I used an old Triang one, purchased a few years ago as a spare. Really this was too large and one about three-quarters the size would have been better, but I had no luck when I tried to find one. So, to complete the model, I used the slightly over-sized one as I did not fancy trying to make my own. The distinctive wide pan to the pantograph was reproduced by soldering a metal strip to the top. It was fixed in place by drilling a central hole in it and the base-plate and bolting firmly with a 6 BA countersunk screw.

Twenty-two seats were cut from the Bec seating strip (obtainable as a spare from the manufacturer) and, after being painted dark brown, they were glued to the appropriate places. The partition at the top of the stairs was made from plastic card and glued into place after painting it brown. Finally, the end seats were made by gluing small blocks of balsa in the floor and covering with plastic card that had been cut to fit the end of the tram and so form the seat. The whole seat was painted brown whilst still in situ. As usual, I then glued some model passengers to the seats. The roof was left off for the moment in order to allow the model to be easily positioned upside down for working on the chassis fittings, other lower saloon details and under-floor parts.

My next problem was how to fit the chassis to the body. I decided that the ends of the chassis gave the best opportunity. The lead weight was removed from the driven end leaving a ready-made hole which was inviting me to use it. So the first job was to remove the strengthening ridges along the edge so that both ends were quite flat. Trying the chassis against the body it was apparent that to keep both parts in line, it was necessary to cut away part of each end to accommodate the recessed doors. This was done using a Junior hacksaw until the chassis dropped into the body in the right place.

Next the drawing was consulted to see how high the bottom of the side should be above the track. By calculating this and allowing for the chassis, I determined that the supports for the chassis needed to be 5½ mm from the bottom edge of the body. They also had to be at the door area to allow sufficient room for the motor and drive unit. Two pieces of $\frac{1}{16}$ in thick wood (not balsa) were cut to fit the width of the body at the doors. These were glued in place so that the bottom was the required distance from the bottom edge of the body. After leaving overnight to set firmly, lines were drawn on the wooden blocks to mark the centre line of the tram. The chassis was placed into the body and the whole lot stood on to some track. The height above the rail was checked as was any tilting from side to side or fore and aft. Some adjustment was needed and I used the flexibility of the impact adhesive to manoeuvre the wooden support into the right place. More glue was then put across the joints. Again it was left overnight to set firmly. I then turned the tram over resting it on the top edge of the sides, allowing me to drop the chassis into position. This was carefully positioned to ensure that it was central and that the bogies were in the appropriate place. The wood below the hole in the chassis was marked with a pencil. A suitable self-tapping screw was found in the bits box and the wood drilled out to suit. Another hole was drilled in the chassis at the other end. The chassis was then temporarily screwed into place at the first end to allow the other end to be marked. The holes drilled, the chassis replaced and fixed using two self-tapping screws. The position and heights were again quickly checked and all was found to be well.

Above *A scratch-built model of a Wolverhampton Corporation combination car by Keith Thompson. This model has been built using plastic card as the main medium and is mounted on a Tenshodo power unit. It is seen running on the Lorraine stud system used so successfully at Wolverhampton (model K. Thompson, photo D. Voice).*

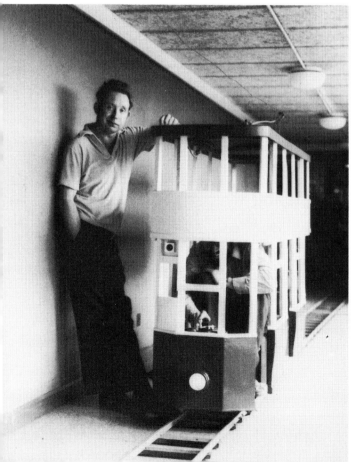

Left *A shade larger than OO gauge is this passenger-carrying tramcar by Richard Wall. He can be seen standing by the model while Dave Watkins takes a break from his Picardy Tramway layout to drive something larger (photo D. Voice).*

So, off came the chassis again and the process of giving a bit of extra weight to the car began. I have some old lead sheet which a friend gave me when he repaired his porchway. This has proved to be ideal for this sort of work. If you are not so lucky, another good method is to use fishermen's lead shot which has been mixed in Plasticine and this allows the weight to be shaped as necessary. In my case, strips were cut from the lead sheet and bent to fit the ends of the tram between the inside of the dash and the wooden support pieces. A piece of plastic card was cut to fit on top of this and painted matt black. When in position it effectively hid the lead weight. Other pieces were cut to fit on the wooden supports and again painted matt black before gluing in place. More lead was added to every part of the chassis which was spare (making sure that it did not affect the fixing of the chassis to the body or the movement of the bogies). All these weights were painted matt black as were the plastic card strengthener, the connecting wires to the motor, and the metal of the body. When all was dry the chassis was fixed back into the body.

The substantial fenders of the tram were made from $\frac{3}{32}$ in thick balsa wood cut to shape using the plan and the actual dash of the model as guides. The prominent rubbing plate on the fender was added from a small piece of thick card. The full thickness was used on the vertical part and it was thinned past the bends by peeling away layers of card until it was only paper thick. Then it was glued in place. The fenders were painted black and rubbed down before giving another coat. This was repeated until a smooth finished was obtained. While this was being done the dog gates on each side were made from thin strip similar to the brass strips used on the body. A sketch was drawn and the gates were made up in the same way as the body was, from the back. I have tried using plastic strip to make gates, as well as lifeguards and trays, as it was a less fiddling way. But they got damaged too easily. The small parts snapped off at the slightest knock. The metal ones are much better. The vertical strips were made twice as long as the depth of the gate and the extra was used to glue the gate in place on the inside of the body. The gates were then painted gloss black. By this time the fenders were ready to be glued into place. Then the step and lifeguards under the fender were soldered up from strips of metal and glued into place. The chassis was removed again and plastic card strips 5 mm wide cut to fit along the inside saloon. The upper parts of the passengers were glued to them making sure that they would not interfere with the position of the motor, bogies or lead weights on the chassis. At this stage it was found that some parts of the 5 mm strip had to be cut slightly narrower. Care was also taken to make sure that the passengers faced the correct direction as the lower deck seats were mostly transverse but had longitudinal seats at the ends. The assemblies were painted dark brown and then the passengers picked out in appropriate colours. A driver was also cut down from a plastic figure and painted in his uniform. These were all then glued into place. The chassis was tested to fit and it was found necessary to cut back a few parts of the seat to allow the chassis to be positioned correctly. It was then removed, given a light oiling and finally screwed into position.

The last details to be added were the destination boxes and the flexible pipes at the ends. I had more or less resigned myself to having just blank destinations as I knew there was no hope of finding a blind reading 'Mumbles Pier'. But on closer inspection of my photos I realised that the other end of the line was, of course, 'Swansea' and a glance at the Mabex catalogue revealed that this was

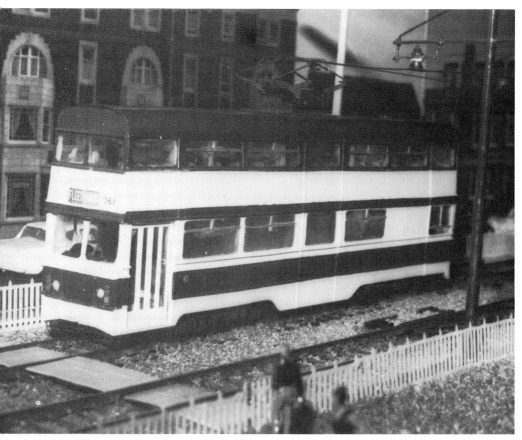

Pride of the Blackpool fleet is the rebuilt tramcar No 761 using all the latest large vehicle technology and breaking into new concepts of tram design. This scratch-built model by Alan Kirkman entered service on his Bispham to Little Bispham layout while the real thing was still undergoing pre-service trials (model A. Kirkman, photo D. Voice).

available as a bus destination. So an order was quickly sent. When I received the transfers back the destination boxes were made up from plastic strip, painted red and the transfer added when the paint was dry. The whole thing was given a couple of coats of varnish and then glued into place above the vestibule. The pipes were bent up from ordinary wire. I had some copper wire that had been varnished with a dark brown colour and this was very suitable, but any bell wire which is plastic coated over a single strand would perform as good a job. Obviously it would be best to get a dark brown or black colour but if not, you could paint the wire after bending but before gluing in place. Finally the roof was fastened in position and the car was ready for its first public showing. I gave it a test run on my small lay-out and was surprised to find that it ran very happily around the 6 in radius curves. However, the very wide vehicle did tend to knock into fixtures on the layout and as a result it had to be banned from one track but with slight adjustments to a horse and cart was able to be run around the other track. The final result has been a car which is most distinctive and which has created a great deal of interest wherever it has been seen.

PART 2: TRAMWAYS
Chapter 8

Layouts

To ensure that your layout does not cause frustration or result in disappointment it is necessary to give sufficient consideration to the design before commencing building. Usually the first thought is how much space is available and this has a major impact on the design. There are other factors such as whether your layout is to be permanently erected or portable, perhaps being only set up at exhibitions and spending the rest of the time in storage. With tram layouts it is possible to build a very satisfying system in the smallest of spaces. My first tram layout, which I still have, was built in a box-file 14½ × 10½ × 3 in and in OO gauge. The purpose of building this layout was partly as a challenge to get as small a layout as possible, but also I intended to have a model which could always stay with me in my moves around the country. But as an operating

I find it difficult to define what I mean by atmosphere in a model layout so I have included this photo which says it all. A corner of Tamebridge, the Black Country layout by Malcolm Till (model and photo M. Till).

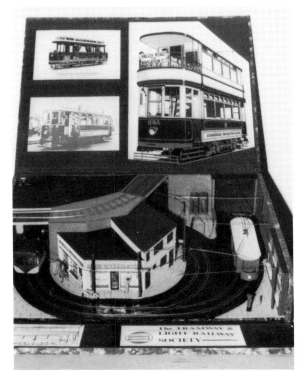

Above *An N gauge end-to-end layout demonstrating the practicalities of modern light rapid transit (the latest jargon for modern trams). This also shows one of the simple layouts for terminals of twin track end to end models* (model Continental Group, photo R. Thomas).

Left *For those who have no room for a tramway, how about this layout in a box file. It is fully operational with working overhead and yet only 14½ × 10½ × 3 in* (model and photo D. Voice).

Top right Diagram 12: *Basic single line end-to-end layouts.*

Above right Diagram 13: *Double line end-to-end layout.*

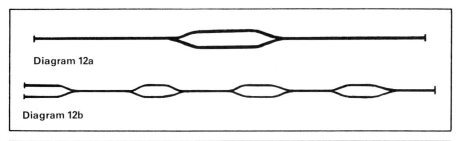

Diagram 12a

Diagram 12b

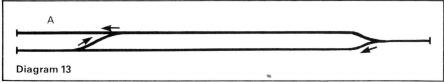

A

Diagram 13

layout it is severely restricted and can only be regarded as a curiosity. This first layout did demonstrate the great advantage in space which trams have over model railways. Most households can be persuaded to have a 6 in wide shelf along one or two walls of a little used room. Such a small space can form the basis of a very realistic and interesting layout.

Before looking in detail at individual layouts it is useful to examine the ideas which need to be clarified before starting. It is then possible to choose the desired basic design from those available. The restrictions on space have already been discussed but it is worth while repeating that you should be quite clear about the space available. Next decide on the main purpose of the layout. It is for exhibition work, for operation with friends, for your own operation, as a test track for your trams, as a photographic back scene for the trams or perhaps to recreate a section, in miniature, of a favourite tram system? Of course, you may wish to combine a number of these or add others of your own. The main purpose of the layout will then define the limitations on the design. For example, in exhibition work the most important considerations are reliable running and interest to visitors. This usually means simple operation and layout design. It is necessary to keep the trams moving or the public soon become bored. However, you may wish, for your own interest, to have a complex system allowing plenty of variety and not be worried by periods of apparent inactivity. If you intend operating it for yourself then only one controller is necessary. If, however, your friends are also going to operate with you then each will wish to participate and have his own controller. It may well be worth considering using the new electronic multiple control systems.

The simplest layout is either a single line going from one point to another or a single oval of track. By using electrical sections more than one tram can be run on the track. However, all the trams must run in the same direction. To allow more trams to be run, and allow either direction to be used, passing loops must be added to the layout. This principle of a single line with passing loops is how the early tramways were built and it will form a good basis for a layout. Diagram 12a shows this simple form with just one passing loop. For longer runs more loops can be added and the terminals can be made more versatile by adding a spur as in Diagram 12b. The next stage is to double the track throughout the length of the run. There are two basic forms of terminus layout and these are shown in Diagram 13. This type of layout is not only more versatile than the previous ones, it also requires less points. Those points which are used can be of the sprung or biased variety. This type of point will accept cars from either track in the trailing direction (that is from the frog end of the point). In the facing direction the tram takes the predetermined direction each time. For example, a loop in a single track can be set so that the tram will always take the left-hand track, therefore allowing approaching cars to pass. The arrows on Diagram 13 show the bias of the points for British operation. The spur 'A' is used to park trams which are not required. Where a reasonable length is available, no matter how narrow, this type of layout is very suitable, particularly for two operators. Each operator takes one end of the line and controls those trams approaching him. This type of design may not be suitable for single-handed operation where it is necessary to keep moving from one end to the other in order to keep the trams moving. This disadvantage can be overcome by using a return loop at one end, as in the first layout to be examined.

Picardy Council Tramways

The return loop design has been used by Dave Watkins in the construction of his layout, Diagram 14. The addition of electrical sections allows up to five trams to be on the layout at any one time. It is more usual for three trams to be operated and the sequence consists of driving a tram from the terminus to the reverse loop followed by a second tram. The final tram follows the second stopping in the section behind it. This clears the terminal spur and allows the first tram to be driven back to the terminus. The second and third trams are moved along a section and the first tram is driven across the crossover freeing the spur for the second tram. The sequence is then repeated. This layout is unusual as it is constructed to EM gauge—that is a track width of 18 mm rather than the more usual 16.5 mm—and this does make the model much more true to scale. Sprung

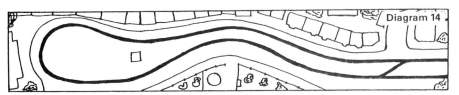

points are used at the terminal thus eliminating any need for point rodding or point motors. The highly detailed scenery and the simplicity and reliability of operation has made this a firm favourite at many exhibitions.

Bispham to Little Bispham

The layout of Alan Kirkman is a more ambitious use of the principle of the return loop, see Diagram 15. A section of the Blackpool Tramway has been created in miniature and, as the name suggests, is based upon the track design at Bispham and Little Bispham. The Blackpool Tramway uses turning circles at not only the furthermost points of Fleetwood and Starr Gate but also at Pleasure Beach and Little Bispham. The latter are used for trams running the short, but busy, journeys along the promenade. The track plan at Bispham is

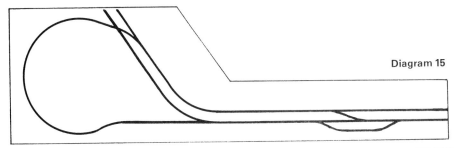

Top of page Diagram 14: *Picardy Council Tramways* (drawing D. Watkins).

Above Diagram 15: *Bispham to Little Bispham.*

Left *The turning circle on the Picardy Council Tramway layout by Dave Watkins. The space in the centre has been imaginatively used to feature a street market* (model D. Watkins, photo D. Voice).

Right *The track at Bispham on Alan Kirkman's Bispham to Little Bispham layout. The 'new' tram to the Blackpool fleet, a rebuild of a 1930s Balloon, No 761 waits in the lay-by loop* (model A. Kirkman, photo D. Voice).

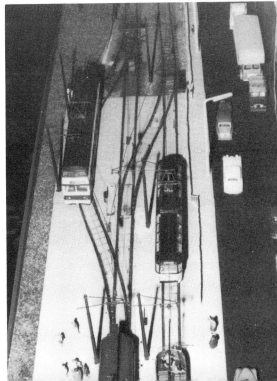

also more complex than is usual on the Blackpool system and this has allowed greater interest in operation of the model. The model has, of necessity, greatly condensed the distance between these two points. The trams which are operated on the layout are those which can be seen and ridden on in Blackpool today. Once again, operating interest has been increased by careful use of sectioning allowing up to eight trams to operate during a hectic session.

Narrow gauge steam trams

The next alternative to the return loop is a layout which allows the trams to go round without need for reversing at any place. In simple terms it is an oval, or some form derived from it. This has been used in its most simple form, that is an oval of single track without points, to make an interesting layout for narrow gauge HOe steam trams. Don Sibley, who has constructed this layout, has used three-quarters of the oval to form the scenic viewing side while keeping the remaining quarter hidden from view to allow the operator to change the locomotives, trailers and wagons. Operation is based upon the steam tramways that used to be so prolific on the Continent. Although, as can be seen from the photographs, the British steam tram has not been ignored. Careful design of the house and shops allows both British and Continental-based models to be equally at home. There are no electrical sections and yet even such a simple design does provide great interest at exhibitions with the steam tram and its train wandering slowly through the market place in front of the shops and round to the blacksmiths and so on to reserved track. In common with all the layouts described in this book a great amount of attention is paid to the scenery to provide the atmosphere which is so necessary in these small layouts. Each creates a miniature scene bringing alive the ideas of each individual modeller.

A narrow gauge (OO₉) steam tram and trailer based on the cars that ran in North London at the turn of the century. Don Sibley's layout is firmly based on the continent yet these British trams do not look out of place (model D. Sibley, photo D. Voice).

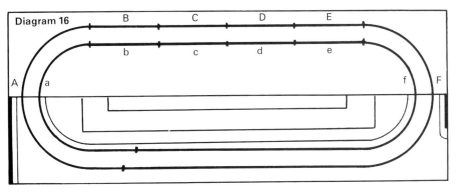

Top Diagram 16: *British United Tramways.*

Above *Looking down the main street of British United Tramways. The scene, at first glance, appears to be pure LCC, however, the museum type running of the layout is revealed by the two farthest trams which are a Leeds Horsfield and a Wolverhampton and District open-top car* (model and photo D. Voice).

British United Tramways

My own exhibition layout, shown in Diagram 16, is simply two concentric ovals. Each oval of track has six sections, four behind the scenes and the other two around each end and meeting by the tram stop at the front. To illustrate how the busiest sequence is operated just one track will be described. It starts with four trams, one each on Sections B, C, D and E—see Diagram 16. The tram from E is driven round the curve under the railway bridge and along the front until it just crosses from Section F to Section A. Here it is stopped and Section A is isolated. The tram from Section D is driven around until it is behind the first tram and halted allowing Section F to be isolated. The tram in Section C is moved to E and that on B to Section D. This allows the first tram to be driven to Section C followed by the second which is parked in Section B. The third tram now in Section E takes its turn to the front stopping just in Section A. It is followed by the fourth tram which stops just behind it but still in Section F. The two trams at the back are moved along the sections as before. The trams in the front are brought around individually to the sections at the back and everything is ready for the sequence to be repeated. With two operators this sequence can be carried out on each oval independently allowing eight trams to be on the layout at one time. Further variety can be introduced by changing trams behind the scenes. Although the operation may seem predictable and repetitive, the variety of trams gives interest to the spectators. Surprisingly, the operators need to concentrate to avoid accidents and seldom get bored. When a rest is required a single tram on each oval is allowed to motor around at a sedate pace.

The Sherwood Tramway

Another layout using the double oval has been built by Michael Funnell. The Sherwood Tramway was built for exhibition purposes and, when not on show, it is stored in the loft. The double track oval goes around a central rectangular box which has a low relief street facade on three sides. The fourth side is used to gain access to the transformer and controllers which are hidden by the box. Again careful sectioning creates extra interest for the viewing public at exhibitions.

Elektrische Tramweg Maatschappij

The oval has also been used as a basis for the HO Continental layout built by Don Sibley. The points on this layout, with the exception of that at A, are all biased as shown in Diagram 17. It is necessary to remember that the

A view of Michael Funnell's layout The Sherwood Tramway. This is another double oval type. Of particular interest are the two nearest trams. The single-deck car is a K's MET Class E, while the balcony car is the Birmingham version of the ready-to-run range once offered by Anbrico. Alas neither of these models is now made (model and photo M. Funnell).

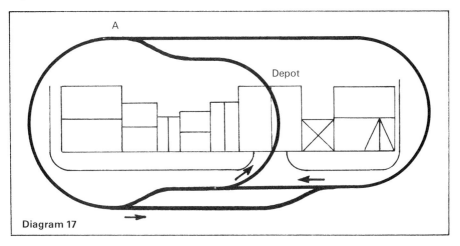

Top Diagram 17: *Elektrische Tramweg Maatschappij.*

Above *Don Sibley has chosen the continent for his HO layout Elektrische Tramweg Maatschappij. Just behind the Birney car can be seen a Ford Anglia with a box on its roof rack. This is a model of the layout itself in transit!* (model D. Sibley, photo D. Voice).

Continental running requires the trams to drive on the right-hand side of the road. The point at A is operated to allow trams to enter or leave the rear of the depot. Up to four trams can be on the layout at any one time. The combination of trolley pole, bow collector and pantograph, all of which need to negotiate the overhead frogs, leads to great visual impact and satisfaction.

Fyldental Bahn

The TT scale (3 mm to the foot) layout owned by the Fylde Tramway Society, and now being restored by Geoffrey Heywood, is also very simple as can be seen in Diagram 18. It is a single track oval of 9 mm gauge track (N gauge) with two passing loops, one on the hidden section and the other on the scenic side. This layout has been built for exhibition work and requires the minimum of

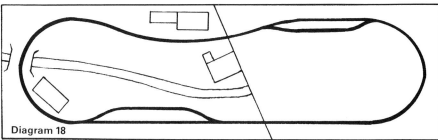

Diagram 18

Top *This TT scale (3 mm to the foot or 1:100) narrow gauge layout is being restored by Geoffrey Heywood. The track is standard N gauge which helps to simplify the modelling, but by necessity the trams and overhead are scratch-built* (model Fylde Tramway Society, photo D. Voice).

Above Diagram 18: *Fyldental Bahn.*

supervision. It is quite incredible to see the tiny trolley poles running along the overhead wire and negotiating the frogs at the passing loops. The visual effect is heightened by the articulated tram which weaves its way around the layout. A layout in such a small scale as this is only recommended to those who have had previous experience, particularly with working overheads. It is best to gain one's skills in a slightly larger scale such as OO or HO. However, this layout does show that tramways can and do work very well even in this small size.

Thatchway Transit
This layout by Wally Sayer uses three, roughly concentric, ovals with a link line between the smallest and the middle lines, Diagram 19. The larger radii of the two outer ovals allows operation of the ready-to-run Continental and American

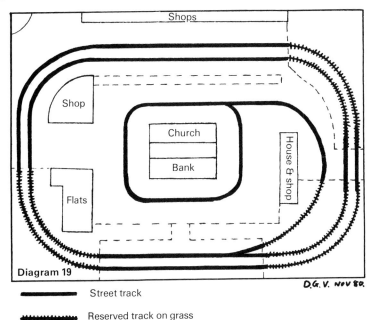

Street track

Reserved track on grass

Top Diagram 19: *Thatchway Transit.*

Above *A busy British scene on Thatchway Transit. This OO gauge layout by Wally Sayer uses three interconnected ovals as its theme. In the background is an articulated Duwag by Roco, obviously on loan from the continent!* (model and photo W. Sayer).

articulated tram models. To enable these and British models to be run on the layout, the design of the buildings has been carefully chosen. This gives a mid-European look allowing British and Continental trams to look equally at home.

Tamebridge

All the layouts described above are fairly small and are all portable. Most appear at various model railway exhibitions near to where the modeller lives. Tamebridge is quite a different type of layout having been built permanently into a room of the home of Malcolm Till. This has allowed a larger and more complex design to be developed, as shown in Diagram 20. Here the basic oval

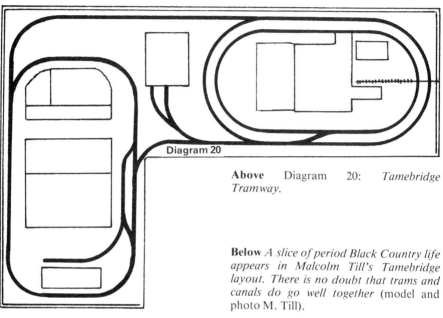

Diagram 20

Above Diagram 20: *Tamebridge Tramway.*

Below *A slice of period Black Country life appears in Malcolm Till's Tamebridge layout. There is no doubt that trams and canals do go well together* (model and photo M. Till).

has been used twice. Once as a single track with passing loops and once as a double oval. The area between the two types of ovals has been used to house the tram depot. The scenery changes from a town shopping centre which is dominated by a large tannery to an industrialised canal basin with warehouses. Sectioning and independent controllers allow a large number of different routes and route combinations to be worked. If Malcolm is working at his bench he can also have the pleasure of seeing a tram riding unsupervised around the tracks. Naturally, a large and complex layout such as this was not built in a few weeks. Work was started on one section and the track laid in the single oval with the passing loop in front of the tannery. A branch was taken from the back of the oval and this was destined to become one of the link lines to the second board. The scenic town was built over many months of enjoyable modelling. When this was completed the second section was started which incorporated those ideas which had been generated during the construction of the first section but which had to be put aside for the lack of available space.

Pontevedro

Another HOe narrow gauge steam tramway has been built by Don Sibley. This layout uses the basic oval with a combination of passing loops. The front half of the layout contains the scenic side while the back half is hidden from all but the operator, as shown in Diagram 21. The bare board is in two pieces hinged several inches above the track height, thus allowing it to be folded into a box with all the rails and scenery well protected inside. Such an arrangement is very

On Don Sibley's Pontevedro layout, a narrow gauge steam tram squeezes under the town gate and past a statue of a local dignitary. The town gate is used to hide the high hinges and framework used at the joint of the two halves of the baseboard (model D. Sibley, photo D. Voice).

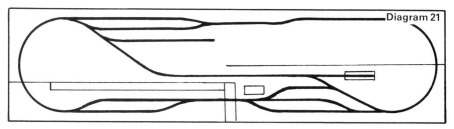

Diagram 21: *Pontevedro.*

convenient but there are always sturdy wood frames and hinges to be hidden at the joint. In this case the difficulty was turned into an opportunity and the town now boasts a medieval style gateway which is a tight squeeze for the trams. Such a feature was not unknown on British tramway networks. For example, Southampton had to have specially designed trams in order to pass through the opening at Bargate. On the layout the town gate naturally forms the break between the urban and rural aspects. One side has the tramway winding its way through the main street of the town. The corner left by the curving road has been used for a quay with an appropriate ship alongside. The rural side shows a more railway-like station with three passing loops, an engine shed and a branch line disappearing behind the station building. The working area behind the back scene is not only used for storing stock and hand shunting but also houses the operating controllers and switches making the whole unit self-contained.

Wolverhampton Corporation Tramways

There is one type of layout design that has not yet been explored and that is the dog-bone, shown in Diagram 22. This is an oval which has been squeezed in the

More Black Country scenes. The viewing section of Keith Thompson's Wolverhampton Corporation Tramways. The lack of overhead is deliberate as the system is modelled during the period when the Lorraine stud contact was used (model K. Thompson, photo D. Voice).

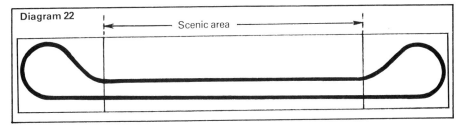

Diagram 22: *Wolverhampton Corporation Tramways.*

middle to give the impression of an end to end layout. Keith Thompson has used this design in his exhibition layout, Wolverhampton Corporation Tramways. The scenic area is restricted to the central part of the layout, showing two tracks along a typical Wolverhampton street. The return loops at each end are normally hidden from view. The two special features about this layout are the automated working and the absence of overhead. By using sections, relays and time delay mechanisms two trams can be operated automatically. This is a useful feature for exhibition work as it allows the operator to put his full attention to discussing tram modelling with the visitors. The absence of overhead is owing to the Wolverhampton system being worked on the surface stud contact type of current supply. Indeed in this respect the Wolverhampton Tramway was the largest installation of this kind in the world and at 20 years it had the longest life. The surface stud and conduit systems allow the modeller of electric tramways to forget the overhead wiring.

In conclusion
The Blackpool Tramway is like a dog-bone layout except the distance between

Tramway modellers always say that tight curves are the rule. However, this old American postcard shows the unbelievably fierce curves that were once used in Philadelphia in the early 1900s. I believe that these caused problems and were eventually removed (D. Voice's collection).

the two end curves is some 12 miles. If this was reproduced in 4 mm scale (OO gauge) the total length of the model would be some 278 yards long. This does illustrate that even though tramways can be built in very small spaces such models only represent a tiny proportion of a real system. There is also a tendency to think that trams are able to go around corners rather than curves. It is true that successful OO gauge tramways have been built with curves as tight as 3 in in radius. However, it is worth bearing in mind that the real tramways generally considered 40ft to be the minimum radius and such curves were the subject of speed restrictions. This scales in OO gauge to about 6 in radius. I have never had any problems with models of British trams on such-sized curves. However, the commercial models of Continental articulated trams require a larger radius and 7½ in is about the minimum. Where small wheelbase four-wheel cars are used the layout can have tighter radius curves but it must be remembered that these models will require a lot of power to negotiate such curves and the track must be laid with particular care. Wherever possible use as large a radius curve as can be fitted in the space available.

Another point which should be considered when contemplating the design of a layout is the provision of means to fit an extension to the layout. One usually finds that once the layout is complete and the operating possibilities are fully explored, one starts to seek further opportunities. With a well thought out layout this can be achieved by adding one or more extension boards. Where such a thing is not practical the only opportunity open is to construct an entirely new layout. In the case of layouts which are built on more than one board the obvious place for extensions is between the existing units. On single board layouts it is useful to build a few extra points where extension lines could be added in order to link with future boards.

Finally a word to all railway modellers. The addition of a tramway to the scenic side of a model railway layout provides an extra interest not only to visitors but also to the operator. As has been shown in this chapter such a feature can be incorporated in a small space, even one which is an awkward shape. To give some ideas I have included a couple of photographs of tramways featured on model railway layouts.

Above left *A continental layout by Helmut Gieramm showing the fine blend of tramway and railway. The models are constructed from the continental range of Bec Kits and are the Hamburg Z1 triebwagen and Z2 beiwagen* (model and photo H. Gieramm).

Left *Another continental layout, this time by the Continental Group, showing the use of a tramway terminus used to hide the fiddle-yard of a railway layout. Operation is automatic* (model Continental Group, photo R.Thomas).

Chapter 9

Track

It requires less effort to roll a metal wheel on metal rails than any other form of vehicle support, other than the hovercraft or the still experimental magnetic levitation. When the concept of the tram, a road vehicle rolling on its own tracks in the highway, was developed the roads were not as we now know them. Most roads were little more than mud tracks. Carriages sank into the mud in winter and raised dust clouds in summer. The surface was, at best, pitted and rutted. Horses could only pull light vehicles with limited passenger-carrying capacity. Even those towns prosperous enough to pave their roads still proved a rough ride and a heavy pull for the horses. On smooth rails with metal wheels a horse could pull a larger, heavier vehicle and, more importantly, a greater number of passengers.

As has been mentioned previously, one of the early pioneers was Mr G.F. Train who had chosen a step rail for his tramways. This rail, shown in Diagram 23a, had, as its name suggests, a raised edge or step some $\frac{5}{8}$ in proud of the road surface. This had a damaging effect on other road traffic and resulted in the London lines being removed within a year of being laid although an earlier line in Birkenhead survived to be re-laid with grooved rail. The use of grooved rail, as in Diagram 23b, did not cause so many problems and was accepted by other road users, although the riders of bicycles always seemed to have problems.

In 1870 the Tramway Act was passed which helped to simplify the development of tramway systems. However, one part of this Act was to have a profound effect on tramway costs and hence profits. It was felt that the horses

Diagram 23: *Tramway Rail.*

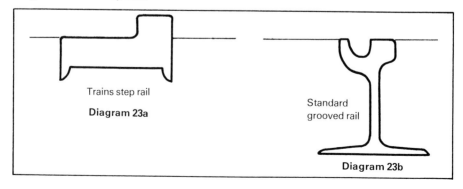

Trains step rail

Diagram 23a

Standard grooved rail

Diagram 23b

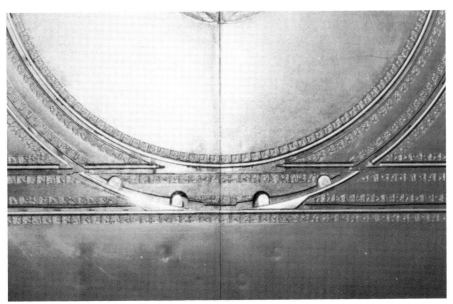

Above *Rivarossi points. At the time of writing this is the only commercially available range of tramway track and points. The road surface is well represented with setts only along the rails. However, the groove is very much over-scale, being made for the deep flanges and wide wheels usually found on commercial ready to run tram models* (photo D. Voice).

Below *Hand scribed setts on a road surface of fire-cement. The groove for the flange is formed using the tool shown in Diagram 25. The tram is the Southport Toast-rack from the latest range by Anbrico* (model and photo D. Voice).

Again the road surface has been hand scribed on fire-cement. This is a part of the Sherwood Tramway by Michael Funnell. The sheen on the road is created and maintained by using black shoe polish (model and photo M. Funnell).

pulling the trams would damage the road surface both between the rails and, to some extent, either side. Therefore, the tramway undertaking was made responsible for the maintenance of the road between the rails and for 18 in on each side. This responsibility never varied and cost the tramway companies dear even when electric traction had seen the demise of the horse. Their bus competitors were running on the roads which the trams were helping to pay for. This law has an effect for the modeller as the road surface often changed depending whether the tram undertaking or the local council was responsible for that particular part.

There were two major track gauges for tramway operators. The standard railway gauge of 4 ft 8½ in and a narrow gauge of 3 ft 6 in. Although the standard gauge appeared to match the railways there is always the substantial difference in wheel flange depth. The groove in the rail was designed for a wheel with a very shallow flange and this had at least two profound consequences. The inspector and regulator of tramways, the Board of Trade, had a ruling (now rescinded) that double-deck tramcars could only run on grooved track, even if it was reserved where no street surface was laid. This rule may seem to have been broken by the Swansea and Mumbles Railway Company. But these very large double-deck vehicles had normal railway depth flanges on their wheels. The second consequence affected those tramway systems such as Glasgow, Huddersfield and Portsmouth where the local railway used to run on the same lines. The large flange wheels of the railway vehicles meant that they rode on the edge of the flange in the groove rather than on the tread of the wheel. The flanges were tapered and, to accommodate them, the tramway track gauge had to be reduced by ¾ in to 4 ft 7¾ in.

The 3 ft 6 in narrow gauge lines were used in towns where street widths were restricted and roads had tight corners and dangerous curves. These trams were narrower than their standard gauge counterparts. Again the Board of Trade affected tram design by preventing any narrow gauge four wheel double-deck tramcar to be totally enclosed. The fear was that the tram could be over-turned in a strong side wind. Thus the four-wheel cars which formed part of the large Birmingham fleet always retained an old fashioned appearance owing to their open balconies.

In modelling the tram track it is normal to adopt the standard track gauges of the model railways. In 4 mm scale (OO gauge) the usual track gauge is 16.5 mm which represents 4 ft 1½ in at full size. Using this size gives the tramway modeller a number of advantages. There is a large variety of material such as wheels and axles, chassis and track, available from model railway shops. The ready-to-run tram models and all the 4 mm British kits are made to run on OO gauge track. The 16½ mm gauge gives a full size width that is nearly halfway between standard and narrow gauges. Therefore, the same track can be used with the same amount of inaccuracy for either gauge. I have run Birmingham (narrow gauge) and London (standard gauge) trams on the same track and no one has objected yet. The purists could use EM gauge track (18 mm gauge) for the standard gauge or a 14 mm gauge track for the narrow gauge. However, the difference in appearance when used in street track is not as noticeable as it is with sleepered railway track. It is recommended that the 16.5 mm track is adopted as this will also allow interchange of models made by different people. It further removes any need to modify commercial chassis or ready-to-run trams. With this in mind the remainder of the chapter will consider OO gauge track as the standard for 4 mm scale modelling.

There is commercially made tram track although it can be rather difficult to find at times. One sometimes comes across the now no longer produced Hamo track. This was made in a variety of lengths and two radii. Hamo also produced points which were made to the smaller radius. The rail was rolled from thin metal and had a very rounded top. This can cause problems for fine scale wheels which tend to ride up and off the rails on the curve and at joints. The original Hamo trams, which were made with very deep flanges, do not suffer from this problem. The track section is quite small and if it is wished to make a realistic street scene it is necessary to build up the road surface on each side. Riverossi also make a street track which consists of modules approximately 8 in square. There are four types, straight, 90-degree curve, point and right-angle crossover. These modules have the whole road width including the pedestrian pavement on either side. The road is very realistic although limited to a single track. The very tight 4 in radius curves do restrict this type of track to the smaller four-wheel tram models.

Most modellers will be making their own street track and the simplest way of achieving this is to use commercially available model railway track and points. To ensure reliable running the rails must be kept clean and with street track it usually means using an abrasive rubber. For this reason I recommend that only solid nickel silver rails are used. The plated type of track soon loses its surface of nickel silver and the bare steel then easily rusts giving very poor running. The extra few pence that the solid nickel silver tracks costs is more than repaid by the length of service one gets from it. The track should be laid on a solidly constructed baseboard. Full descriptions on this type of construction can be found in the *PSL Model Railway Guide No 1* by Michael Andress on baseboards, track and electrification. Where flexible railway track is used on curves which have a radius of less than 1 ft it is advisable to slide out the rails and bend them to roughly the radius required, being careful to keep the curve smooth and easing out any kinks which may form. The rails should be slid back into the plastic chairs and the track laid on the baseboard and pinned into place according to the layout diagram. The rails should be cut through with a fine saw at all electrical section breaks. The gap so formed should be filled with a small piece of plastic card glued into place and smoothed when set. It is useful at this stage to cut as many sections as is thought will ever be needed. It is far easier to eliminate a section no longer required by soldering a connecting wire across the gap than it is to cut a new section on a piece of track built into the road surface. The golden rule is always cut all the sections you think you will ever need. When all the track is laid the street surface can be built around it. There are a number of different methods available. Plastic card, either plain or embossed with brickwork, can be carefully cut and laid between, and either side of, the rails as in Diagram 24. Notice that the rails have been left proud of the surface to facilitate track cleaning. Laying the plastic card is a fiddling job which must be carried out as neatly as possible to create the desired effect. The main disadvantage of this method, where embossed plastic card is used, is that it does not look correct on the curves. This can be overcome by using the special embossed plastic card produced specifically for tram street tracks by the Loughborough Model Shop. There are two types produced for straight or curved track, but no similar product is available for point-work.

Alternatively, the road surface can be constructed using either plaster or one of the modelling clays. Plaster tends to be very dusty and must be sealed with paint when the street is completed. The modelling clays do not have this problem and I have used them most successfully in creating street scenes. Fill the area between the rails first. The modelling clay is rolled and smoothed until the surface lies just below the top of the rail. The amount of modelling clay used can be considerably reduced by laying pieces of card on the sleepers before covering with clay. While the clay is hardening off use the tool shown in Diagram 25 to form the groove for the wheel flanges. Any type of metal is suitable for this tool which is easily made by sawing the slot for the rail with a hacksaw. If necessary give a few cuts with the hacksaw blade at an angle to enlarge the slot until it is a snug fit over the rail. The clay should be removed a little at a time, wiping the tool clean on each occasion. When this is complete the surface can be marked to represent the stone setts. It is not practical to attempt to make these exactly to scale. Like many aspects of modelling the road surface is an area where a little exaggeration enhances the viewer's perspective rather than detracting from the model. I find that setts made approximately 4 mm long and 2 mm wide appear true to scale. Mark a series of lines with a curved bladed craft knife across from one rail to the other at 2 mm intervals. When the section of clay has been fully marked in this way the individual setts are picked out using the point of the craft knife to give an overlapping pattern of the type seen in modern brickwork. This should be left for about 48 hours to harden. The special tool should be run along each groove to remove any odd pieces of clay which may be stuck in it. Now the street either side of the rails can be made up using the same procedures. It is worth while spending a little extra time to create some of the distinctive patterning of the setts. For example there was often a line

Above *This view of Dave Watkins' Picardy layout shows the home made glassfibre road surface and the black plastic card strip used to form the inner edges of the groove* (model D. Watkins, photo D. Voice).

Below Diagram 24: *Street track construction using plastic card surface.*

Bottom Diagram 25: *Road formed from modelling clay.*

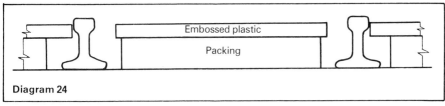

Embossed plastic

Packing

Diagram 24

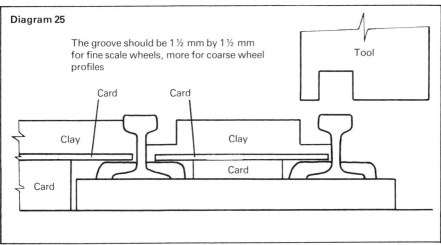

Diagram 25

The groove should be 1 ½ mm by 1 ½ mm for fine scale wheels, more for coarse wheel profiles

Tool

Card   Card

Clay   Clay

Card

Card

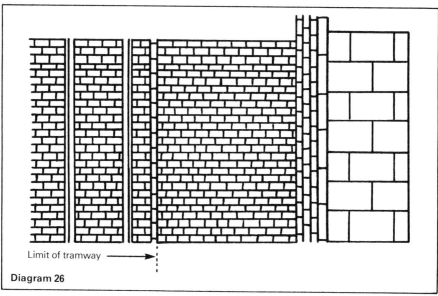

Limit of tramway ────→

Diagram 26

of setts at right angles to the rest some 18 in from the rails showing the limit of responsibility of the tramway company. The gutter by the pavement was also laid at right angles usually with three rows of setts. Diagram 26 illustrates these patterns. A realistic effect which is somewhat simpler to build can be achieved by only marking setts on that part of the road which was the responsibility of the tramway company, leaving the remainder smooth to represent tarmacadam. When the road surface has been completed and allowed to dry thoroughly it should be painted the desired colour. I prefer a dark grey/blue colour (Humbrol

Left *Don Sibley has used a nickel silver strip, Diagram 28a, to form the groove. The road surface is scribed plaster* (model D. Sibley, photo D. Voice).

Below left Diagram 26: *Pattern of setts in street track.*

Right *A point complex outside the depot at Crich. Note that on the nearest point there is only one moving blade while the next point has two moving blades. Also the setts are smaller, in proportion, than those scribed on layouts. In my view the overscale setts on the models actually enhance the effect* (photo D. Voice).

No HM5) which has been thinned with an equal volume of thinners.

On point-work the same techniques are used except that the moving parts of the blade mechanism must be left completely free of clay. Lay card over the moving tie-bar to prevent the clay fouling the moving parts. Fill other areas which are to be left free of clay with Blu-Tac. Apply the modelling clay as before, forming the groove and marking the setts. When all is hardened the Blu-Tac can be removed allowing the point to operate freely. Connect the point to a point motor or hand lever by any of the means available to the model railway maker. The use of live frog points is recommended as they are less prone to causing trams to stall. There seems to be a mystique about this type of point but, in practice, the guidance given by the manufacturers is quite clear and simple. If these instructions are carried out there are no mysteries to this useful type of point. However, there are two major disadvantages in using these commercial points. They are really made for model railway use and do not have the small radius curves which are more tram-like. The smallest radius that you will find will be between 18 in and 24 in. On the point itself there are two large lengths of rail which need to move and the tram points really only had one small blade. The next part of this chapter will concentrate on methods of making your own track and points thus eliminating these disadvantages.

The previous method of obtaining street track relied upon a groove being cut in the clay to represent the groove in the actual tracks. When painted this did deceive the eye of the onlooker and the over-scale groove did not appear obtrusive. There are many other ways that can be used to represent this groove which include methods of allowing the lip and sometimes the whole of the groove to be formed in metal. The most straightforward is the use of a continuous check rail, as shown in Diagram 27a. There is some made as a flexible track, manufactured by Shinohara, that can be purchased in specialist model shops. However, with the advent of copper-clad sleepers the prospect of making your own track has become more attractive. The rail is soldered on the

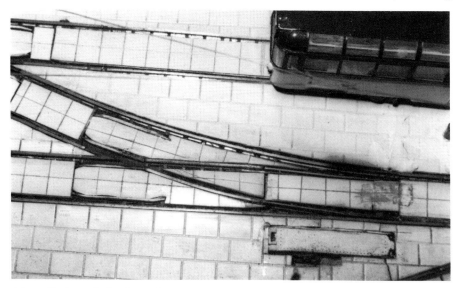

Above *Embossed plastic card is used on Alan Kirkman's layout to represent the paving slabs used at Blackpool. The point is from the model railway market and the plastic has been laid to ensure free movement of the point* (model A. Kirkman, photo D. Voice).

Right Diagram 27: *Track and point construction using continuous check rail.*

Below *Only the inner parts of the London tramway system ran on conduit. The outer suburbs were fitted with the less costly overhead supply. For the trams to move from one part to the other these distinctive features were required and were called change pits. This one is at Longley Road, Merton. Each was manned by a ploughman who, no matter what the weather, removed the ploughs from outgoing cars and fitted them to ingoing vehicles. The tops of ploughs can be seen above the slot of the conduit* (photo W.J. Hayes).

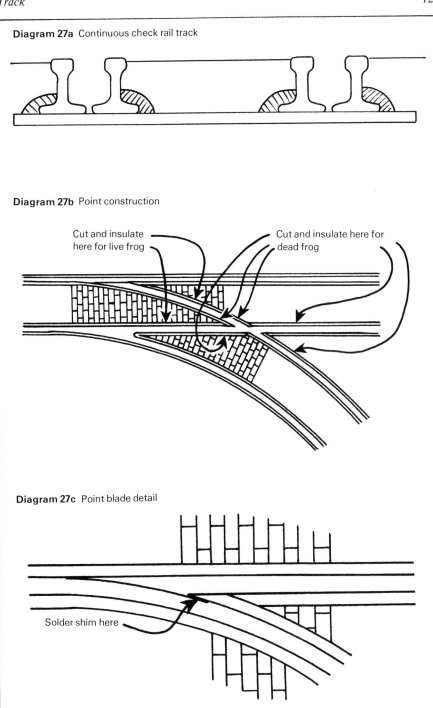

Diagram 27a Continuous check rail track

Diagram 27b Point construction

Cut and insulate here for live frog

Cut and insulate here for dead frog

Diagram 27c Point blade detail

Solder shim here

Diagram 27

outside to the copper cladding on the sleepers and therefore the inside edge has no protrusions and a smaller rail section can be used even for the coarse wheels of commercial models. The use of Code 80 rail, which is normally found on N gauge track, becomes a practical proposition. This size rail is easily found and proves ideal for this purpose. Solder one rail to a series of sleepers. Since it is not intended to create railway track and the sleepers will be covered by road surface they need only be positioned at approximately 1 in intervals. This sub-assembly is then laid on the baseboard to the required shape. Pin into place with small nails or even temporarily with drawing pins. Using a track gauge, solder the second rail into place. If you wish to use coarse scale wheels on very tight curves it is useful to open the track gauge to 17 mm. Where the intention is to operate trams on a two-rail electrical supply, or to use each rail as an independent feed with a common return through the overhead, it is useful to ensure that the sleepers are bought with a gap already made in the copper cladding. Otherwise such a gap will have to be cut with a sharp craft knife. Run a selection of models over the track in order to ensure that all is well. Solder the check rail into place using a small piece of wood or cardboard as a spacer. These should be 1½ mm thick for the straights and 1¾ mm for the curves. Again check the track by running trams. If necessary re-position the check rail at any places which appear to be troublesome. When you are completely satisfied that the track is without fault then the sections should be cut, appropriate wires soldered to each section and the road can be built up as before. In this case there is no need to cut the grooves.

Points are made in a similar fashion using the longer sleepering available for this purpose. The frog should be made by filing the rails to shape and soldering them together at the correct angle. This is easily obtained by first drawing the desired point and then laying the rails on the appropriate parts of the diagram and soldering together. The frog should be soldered to the sleepers and then the straight rail soldered in the appropriate place checking the track gauge at the frog. The next rail is curved to the correct shape making sure the curve is true. Solder the rail to the sleepers checking at the frog and at the blade with the track gauge. Cut all the smaller rails and the check rail to length and curve and file as necessary before soldering in place on the sleepers, as shown in Diagram 27. Make sure that the appropriate insulation is in position if the system is running on two-rail. If you are using an overhead supply with the electrical return through both rails then there is no need to incorporate any insulation. The blade is simply a piece of thin brass shim cut to the height of the rail and soldered as shown in Diagram 27c. On tramway points there need only to be one blade and the operation of the points is virtually invisible. It is useful to connect the operating wire to a double pole single throw switch to change the electrical polarity of the live frog as necessary. This, of course, is not required where the live overhead is being used. For automatic bias points on two rail layouts it will be necessary to use a dead frog point as shown in the diagram. In this case the operation of the points does not preclude trams from running into the points from the 'wrong' (trailing) direction. The brass shim blade does not impede the travel of the tram and the flanges on the wheels just ride up over the blade and drop back into the groove with only a slight rocking of the tram. The point can now be placed on the layout and the appropriate road surface made up as before.

The use of the continuous check rail does not produce an entirely correct

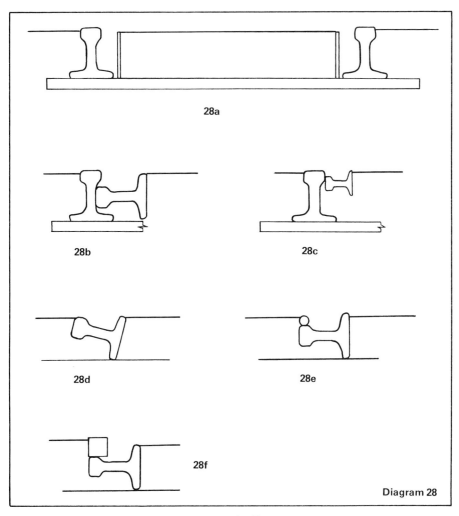

28a

28b

28c

28d

28e

28f

Diagram 28

Diagram 28: *Methods of reproducing grooved rail.*

representation of grooved tram tracks. A better alternative is to use a continuous strip, such as in Diagram 28a. I have seen two forms of this used very successfully. Don Sibley has used nickel silver strip $\frac{1}{16}$ in wide and .010 in thick. This is used in the same way as described previously except the nickel silver strip replaces the check rail. Being metal it can easily be soldered to the copper-clad sleepers. More usefully it is much easier to handle and curve. David Watkins used a strip of similar size but his was in black plastic card. This was glued in the appropriate place. It is interesting to compare the photographs of the two layouts. In the case of Don Sibley the road surface has been built up using plaster which was smoothed and scribed to represent the setts when it had dried. David Watkins made his own road surface using a mould he constructed from Plasticine and making small sheets of road surface using glass fibre and resin and curing the whole lot in an ordinary domestic cooker. The home-made sheets were then cut and positioned as described at the beginning of this chapter.

Left *An original Lorraine stud removed from the tram depot at Wolverhampton and now on view at Crich (photo D. Voice).*

Below left *The Lorraine stud system in model form by Keith Thompson. The road surface is the commercially available embossed plastic card specifically made for tram track (model K. Thompson, photo D. Voice).*

Below *Complex track and sett patterning on this depot which is part of the Idleburg layout by Noel Dollimore. The track is hand constructed and despite its scale appearance, it will accept the coarser size commercial tram wheels (model N. Dollimore, photo D. Voice).*

Another method of achieving a realistic groove is to use a second rail laid at right angles inside the normal running rail. Diagram 28b shows one form using two Code 100 rails. The second rail is laid with its head in the web of the first rail. The edge of the flat bottom forms the edge of the groove. This method produces a groove which is a little wide. A closer to scale effect can be obtained by using the same method with a Code 65 rail for the check rail, as shown in Diagram 28c. This in turn has led to consideration of the use of a Code 65 rail laid with a slight tilt on its side, as shown in Diagram 28d. However, experiments have shown that even the finest scale wheels have too deep a flange for such a shallow groove. The tram runs along the edges of the flange rather than the surface of the wheel. This causes electrical conductivity problems and results in erratic running. This can be solved by soldering a 20 swg (.036 in) copper wire to the edge of the rail head as in Diagram 28e. In practice this is a tricky job as the soft wire kinks very easily and the result is not as acceptable as the theory suggests. This problem can be resolved by using a $\frac{1}{32}$ in square section nickel silver strip. This is soldered in the same manner as the wire and is shown on Diagram 28f. Points are constructed in much the same manner as before except that at the blade end the rails need to be cut lengthways in order to accommodate the track divergence and the brass shim blade.

At the same time as the road surface is constructed the pavement kerbing and smaller details like drains and ramps can be added. After painting with matt enamel, the appropriate degree of variety can be brought out by using water colour paints applied vigorously with a stiff brush, such as an old tooth brush. This has a great advantage as the degree of colour variation can be controlled very finely and, if it is felt that it has been over-done in any part, the excess paint is easily removed with a damp cloth.

There were two types of electrical supply for trams which did not use the overhead wire. These relied on equipment embedded in the road surface and were the conduit and surface stud contact. Conduit systems were used in Blackpool and Bournemouth for short periods but the most famous user was London County Council. In the central areas of London it was considered desirable to have the streets free from overhead wiring and so a very extensive, and expensive, conduit system was used. In the suburbs this was not considered worth while and the economy of the overhead system was favoured. This led to that most distinctive feature, the 'change pit' where the plough was either removed or attached to the plough-carrier on the tram and the trolley pole raised or lowered as required. The conduit system is an attractive proposition for the modeller as it does remove the necessity of having overhead wiring which at times can be a little fiddling to construct.

The conduit itself can easily be represented by fixing Peco rail of the same code number as the running rails in the centre of the track but upside down, as shown on Diagram 29a. It is necessary to use Peco rail as this is made with a groove along the centre of the base. This groove looks just like the slot in the conduit system. To attach the rail it should be soldered to brass nails hammered into the baseboard. The road surface should be built up as described previously. It is not recommended that this centre rail is used for electrical pick-up purposes. Rather, the running rails should provide a two-rail type of supply.

The surface stud contact system was used at various times in London, Hastings, Lincoln, Torquay and Mexborough. But the most famous and long lasting was the Lorraine system in Wolverhampton. This survived many years

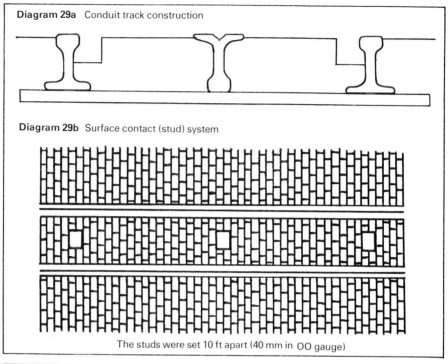

Diagram 29a Conduit track construction

Diagram 29b Surface contact (stud) system

The studs were set 10 ft apart (40 mm in OO gauge)

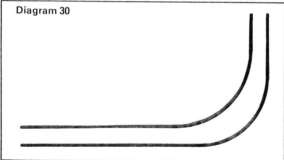

Diagram 30

Above Diagram 29: *Conduit and surface contact (stud) track construction.*

Left Diagram 30: *How to increase the distance between tracks on curves to prevent collisions.*

and some of the actual studs, recovered from one of the depots, have been laid on a section of track at the National Tramway Museum, Crich, to demonstrate this type of electrical supply. In model form studs can be represented by small nails or even pieces of card suitably cut, painted and glued onto the road surface (Diagram 29b). Once again it is recommended that the actual electrical supply to the model trams would be through the two-rail system.

General considerations

Keep the width of double track sufficient to allow two of your widest cars to pass without risk of collision. It is recommended that the minimum gap between centres of the tracks should be 1½ in. If central traction poles are used then this should be increased to at least 2 in. Do not forget that trams have considerable over-hang at the ends and these measurements will need to be increased on the curves. One method of preventing collisions on curves is shown in Diagram 30. It is useful to check the running characteristics of your track at every stage. That is, as soon as it is laid, with the road surface built up between the rails and the groove formed, and then with the complete road surface laid. Do not go from one stage to the next until you are satisfied with the way that all your trams run on the track. I have often found a tight spot on a curve which has been easy to rectify before the road was laid but which would have caused serious problems had that part of the scenic work been completed.

Make sure that you have decided on all the sections you will want when doing your track plans. Cut each one as the rail and track are laid. Where there is any doubt, put in a section break. To reiterate previous comments in this chapter, it is easy to wire across a section break and nearly impossible to create a section in a finished street. This is a most important consideration for full enjoyment of your layout.

Throughout the design and construction of the layout keep track cleanliness in mind. All road surfaces should be kept slightly lower than the top surface of the rail. This helps to preserve both the painted surface of the road during cleaning and makes the cleaning of the track surface a less laborious task. Care in the design and provision of traction poles for overhead support will also enable access to the track to be more convenient.

Chapter 10

Overhead

In the early days of the development of the electric tram there were many and often ingenious solutions to the problem of getting the electricity to the tram. The first electric street tramway to operate in this country, at Blackpool, used the conduit system mentioned in the previous chapter. However, operators soon found that the overhead wire with a trolley pick-up was the most reliable, simplest and least expensive system. Unless there were other factors, such as objections on aesthetic grounds, the overhead wire was the system chosen. In common with many other features of the tramway construction and operation the regulations were applied by the Board of Trade. For example, the minimum height of the wire from the road surface was 20 ft except in special circumstances, such as low bridges, where the Board of Trade inspector could vary the regulations but usually within strict limits and possibly subject to other special rules.

Span wire overhead on the Sherwood Tramway. This model system is scratch-built including the ears and traction poles (model and photo M. Funnell).

The overhead is held up by traction poles which are spaced no more than 120 ft apart, and often less. In the early days the poles were decorated with ornate iron scroll-work, although later the need for economy made the poles very much simpler in design. There are three main types of traction pole, the simplest being the span wire one. Here the poles are quite plain and a span wire is placed between pairs of poles set either side of the track. The overhead wire (or wires) is hung from this span wire. A little more complex is the bracket arm pole where the single pole has an arm projecting over the tracks, the overhead wires are slung from this arm. Sometimes this arm is very long in order to reach tracks in the centre of the road. The size then varies to the very short arm where the trolley pole on the tram has to reach for the overhead wire. The most complex is the centre pole where the traction pole is mounted between the tracks and a bracket arm projects from either side. These poles were installed in the roadway with no traffic island or any other protection, but the road speeds and traffic density were not as high as today.

A hanger is fitted to the arm or span wire and an ear is attached to the hanger. The overhead wire is then clamped to the ear to form the complete assembly. In the model form the hanger and ear are usually considered as a single entity and may be referred to by either name. For the sake of uniformity I will use the term 'ear' to mean this assembly.

At points and crossings special equipment is required. To allow the trolley pole to follow the correct overhead wire when the tram passes a facing point there is an overhead frog. Where there is a divergence of tracks, as in this case, the frog has a moving blade which ensures that the wheel or skid on the trolley pole is directed correctly. In the case of points which are biased in one direction the frog blade is sprung in the preferred direction, and for points which are only used in the trailing direction the frog may not need a blade. In the case of

Span wire overhead in O gauge using the Meadowcroft system. The railway bridge is used to disguise the joint between baseboads (model P. White, photo D. Voice).

Left *A bracket arm traction pole in OO gauge. This and the ear is from the Meadowcroft range. Note also the use of pull-off wire to allow the trolley wire to follow the curve of the track* (model A. Kirkman, photo D. Voice).

Below left *Part of a static display with very long bracket arms showing detailed scrollwork. This was made in OO gauge to represent a section of road and overhead of the Exeter system. A span wire tapered traction pole from Meadowcroft was used and the bracket arm and scrollwork were scratch-built. The ears are from the Suydam range* (model and photo D. Voice).

Below *Centre track, double bracket arm traction poles from the Sommerfeldt range. The articulated tram is a combination of two Bec Brussels PCC kits mounted on a Roco chassis* (model and photo H. Gieramm).

Below right Diagram 31: *Traction poles on a curve.*

Below far right Diagram 32: *Scroll and scroll jig.*

current collection systems which use a bow or pantograph exclusively there is no need for these complexities. Where the collection is mixed with trolley poles and pantographs or bows, the frogs must be able to provide a smooth passage to the sliding pans. At crossings the arrangements are very similar except that the overhead crossing does not require any moving blades.

Complete systems are available to the modeller. One which has been out of production for some time, but is occasionally found, is the Hamo range. This is only suitable for single-deck HO tramways as the height above the rail is only 65 mm, far too low for the double-deck OO tram. However, the system is most ingenious allowing simple erection and dismantling time after time. It is not suitable for trolley pole operation. Currently available is the Riverossi system designed specifically for use with the track sections in the same range. This system is rather overscale and, again, does not give sufficient height for British OO models. A system which is very much more to scale is that marketed by Sommerfeldt and available in some specialist model shops. It is, however, rather expensive and again below the OO scale height requirement of 80 mm. However, it does complement the range of ready-to-run Continental and American tram models. In all cases of currently manufactured items instructions on the use of the systems are available from the manufacturers.

When modelling the overhead my aim is to make a system which looks as much like the real thing as possible while being reliable in use and having enough strength to withstand the occasional accidental knock. In 4 mm scale, traction poles can be obtained from Meadowcroft models. These are turned from steel rod in the stepped taper style so common to British traction poles. The lower part is threaded for fixing purposes. The baseboard is drilled with a drill having the appropriate clearance, the drill being held as near to vertical as possible. If the material covering the baseboard is fibreboard, or any similar soft material, it is useful to glue squares of pre-drilled plywood above and below the hole in order to form a firm anchorage. If the layout is large enough the traction poles can be set the scale 120 ft apart, which is some 18 in. It is usual to place them nearer at 9 in to 12 in, which creates the illusion of a longer stretch of track as well as providing greater strength. On curves the prototype has many

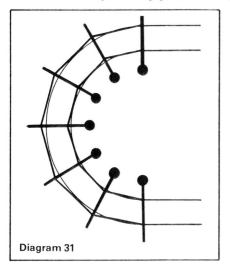

Diagram 31

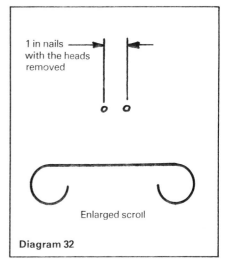

1 in nails with the heads removed

Enlarged scroll

Diagram 32

Left *Close-up of a Meadow-croft ear. The trolley wire is threaded through the ear and soldering is not necessary in this system. The ear is fully insulated from the traction pole* (photo D. Voice).

Below Diagram 33: *Types of ears.*

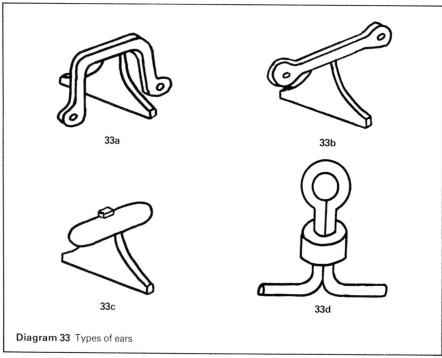

33a

33b

33c

33d

Diagram 33 Types of ears

traction poles with a multiplicity of span wires to ensure that the angle at each ear does not cause the trolley pole to de-wire. In the model form the tolerances allow far more acute angles and this, with a little cheating by curving the wire slightly, can reduce the number of traction poles required. For example, on curves of 6 in to 9 in radius only four poles are needed for a right-angle or seven for a semi-circle, as shown in Diagram 31. In the prototype the span wire type of overhead gained favour for its versatility and easy maintenance. However, in model form the single side bracket traction pole is recommended for a number of reasons. It is stronger than the span wire and also allows the modeller to show off his skills on the scroll-work. Most importantly, the single bracket arm type of overhead can, when positioned correctly, allow the operator access to the track for cleaning and other maintenance purposes and enables him to retrieve (or encourage with a slight push) stubborn trams. For variety it is nice to include some span wire and possibly centre poles where there is otherwise clear access to the track.

Mark out on the layout the position and type of each traction pole and, if desired, construct the side arm poles. These can be obtained ready-made from Meadowcroft Models. In making your own, the side arm is made from piano wire cut to the full length required. It is pushed through the small hole in the traction pole and held in position by a touch of solder. The main support stays from the top of the pole to the arm are made from nickel silver or brass wire twisted in place at the end and secured by solder. The small drop stays on the bracket arm, which will support the ears, are made in a similar way. Scroll-work is formed from copper wire, 15-amp fuse wire being ideal. The small scrolls at the crossover of span arm and pole are easily mass-produced using the jig shown in Diagram 32. Two nails are fixed into a block of wood and the heads cut off. The wire is wound one turn around a nail then across to the next nail and given a turn around it and then back to the first nail and so on. Using a sharp knife with a strong blade cut straight up the inside edge of both nails. When the wire is removed you will find lots of identical scroll pieces ready to be fitted into place. Larger or more elaborate scroll-work may need to be made individually using pliers and tweezers. To assist assembly, use a block of wood with a groove cut in it which is as deep as half the diameter of the traction pole. On the wood draw the span arm in place and then draw all the scroll-work. Lay the traction pole in the groove with the span arm lying over its place on the drawing. Secure the pole in place with some adhesive tape at its base. Position the scroll-work on the drawing and solder the parts in place. It is advisable to use tweezers to hold the wire in place as it all gets very hot. I have found that the easiest way is to fix one end of the scroll in the right place while holding the other end roughly in position. Then the wire can be adjusted slightly to get it exactly in the right position and shape before soldering the other end. Although it all sounds complicated in practice it is quite easy. After a little experience you will be able to make an elaborate pole which will look most impressive. The general idea is to make up all the poles and then choose the neatest for the most prominent places on the layout and put the less good ones towards the back or behind the scenes. After soldering, wash the poles thoroughly in water to which you have added detergent. Allow them to dry completely and then give two coats of paint and finish with some varnish. The colour of traction poles did vary from one system to another but, if you have difficulty in determining which is correct, I suggest you use dark green (Humbrol Gloss No 31) as this was the most favoured colour in the country.

There are two main types of ear commercially available. The first uses an insulated collar and an ear soldered to a threaded screw and this is part of the Meadowcroft system, while the other type is made by Suydam and is a lost wax brass casting. The former uses brass shim for the ear which wraps around the overhead wire. If this type is used there are comprehensive instructions available from the manufacturer. The cast ears are quite different and as no instructions are given, I will go into detail about their use. There are three types available, see Diagram 33; one of which is suitable only for trolley pole operation. The

Above *The traction poles on this continental layout are from the Rivarossi tramway system, although the remainder of the overhead is scratch-built* (model and photo H. Gieramm).

Below *A prototype trolley reverser, now preserved at Crich. This shows the cobweb of wires necessary* (photo D. Voice).

other two can be used for trolley, pantograph or bow. Clean the top of each casting, cutting the casting spigot short if required. Types 'a' and 'b' (Diagram 33) are fixed by threading thin wire through the hole and twisting to reach the stays on the traction pole arm or in the case of span wire from one pole to the other. In the case of type 'c' wire should be wound around the top of the ear and touch-soldered to make it secure. The ears should be attached to the side arm type of traction pole before positioning it on the layout. As the ear assembly is best secured to the traction pole by solder it is best to leave the painting until the whole assembly is complete. The span wire type is best painted before attaching the ears as the assembly must be done on the layout.

It is possible to make your own ears. Where a layout uses only pantographs or bows it is quite acceptable not to use ears and instead solder the overhead wire directly to the cross wires. Where ears are desired or made necessary by trolley pole operation, they can be made using short lengths of brass tubing or small glass beads. An old necklace can be the source of enough beads for a complete layout. The assembly is shown in Diagram 33d. This type of construction can also be achieved without the tube or beads but it is not as visually satisfying. These home assembled ears are used in the same way as the commercially available types.

The position of the overhead wire on the layout will depend on the needs of the trams. When pantographs or bow collectors are to be used the overhead wire must lie over the centre of the track, give or take a few millimetres. For trolley-only operation the wire should be placed over the inner rail on bends. This style was used particularly with fixed-head trolley poles where the top of the pole needs to be at a tangent to the curve of the wire.

At this stage you should have the traction poles in place on the layout, and the ears fixed to the traction poles or attached to the span wires between plain poles. All that is needed to complete the assembly is the overhead wire itself. This can be made from either piano wire, copper wire or nickel silver wire. The piano wire will give a very strong overhead that will not expand under heat and will resist kinking which might occur if accidentally knocked. Therefore, it is very suitable for portable layouts used in exhibitions. However, piano wire is very poor for electrical supply and the two-rail method should be used. Where the overhead is used for electrical supply, copper or nickel silver wire must be used. The wire chosen should be straightened as much as possible and all kinks removed. With copper wire this is easily done by fixing one end to a strong point and giving the other end a few sharp tugs until the wire stretches slightly and becomes straight. Starting at an overhead frog position or at the back of the layout or any other place where there is a natural break or the overhead wire is hidden, solder the wire to the first ear. When you begin you will find that a third hand is necessary. However, with practice the soldering iron can be held in one hand while the wire is held taut with the thumb and third finger while the fore-finger positions the wire on the other side of the ear to enable the soldering to be done. This is all made easier if the underside of the ear and the approximate location on the wire are tinned with solder before bringing them together. Then just a quick wipe along with the soldering iron will give a good strong point.

Pull the wire gently until reasonably taut and solder it to the next ear. Repeat this procedure until the whole overhead is secure or until a frog is reached. The model overhead frog need not be as complicated as the real thing. There is no need to worry about any moving parts. In fact it is probably best to spend the

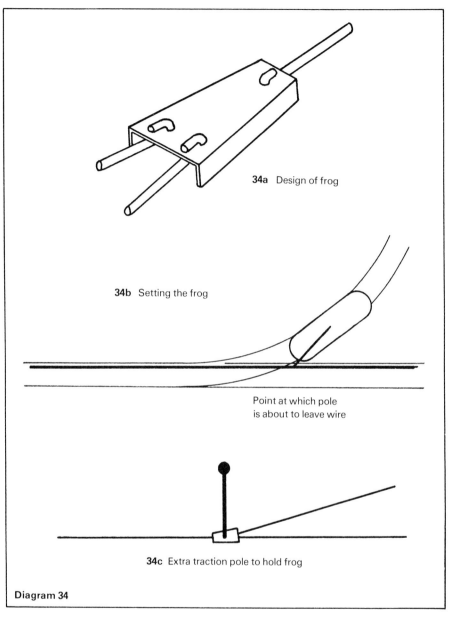

34a Design of frog

34b Setting the frog

Point at which pole
is about to leave wire

34c Extra traction pole to hold frog

Diagram 34

small amount required and purchase your frogs ready-made from either Meadowcroft or at a model shop stocking Suydam parts. They are made to operate with the manufacturer's trolley heads, so make sure your fleet is adapted to that size and shape. Diagram 34a shows the construction of the frog and can be followed if you wish to make your own using shim brass. The overhead wires are fixed to the frog by threading through the holes and bending over at the top. For added strength a spot of solder can be placed over the wire and top of the frog. This type of frog depends for its operation on the angle at

Left Diagram 34: *Frogs and their setting.*

Right *This overscale frog from the Rivarossi range shows the features necessary. See also Diagram 34a* (photo D. Voice).

Below *The model trolley reverser on the Picardy Tramway. Using the stiffness of the model trolley wire has allowed a drastic reduction in the support necessary* (model D. Watkins, photo D. Voice).

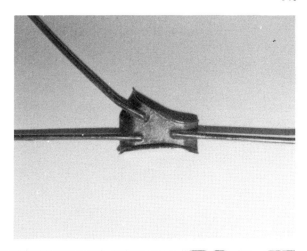

which the trolley head is drawn under the pan of the frog. Therefore, to give it maximum opportunity it should be placed where the difference in angles, depending on which route is taken, is greatest without incurring the risk of de-wiring the trolley pole. Lay the overhead wire along the straight route temporarily, slightly to the side where the other route turns off. Try your tram using the one with the least reach on its trolley poles. Push this over the curved route until the trolley pole is close to being pulled off the wire, as shown in Diagram 34b. The frog should be placed just before this position. As a check

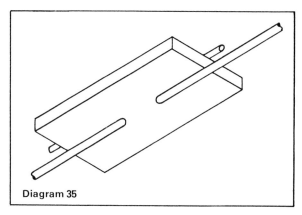

Diagram 35

Left Diagram 35: *Overhead wire joint, plastic for insulated joints and metal for non-insulated.*

Right *A cobweb of overhead is not always confined to the prototype. Here a complex track junction requires an equally complex overhead* (model and photo H. Gieramm).

you should find that this is somewhere close to being directly over the frog of the track point. Cut the wire and fix the overhead frog in place. Fix the other two wires on to the frog and so to the next ears. Now thoroughly test all your trams on the overhead. If there are any problems adjust the position or angle of the frog. In very awkward situations where the positioning of the frog seems critical, place an extra traction pole by the frog in order to hold it firmly in place as in Diagram 34c. On a layout which is built to accommodate pantograph or bow collectors as well as trolley poles, the positioning of the frogs must also take account of the needs of the other types of pick-up. If the frog is placed too far to either side the skid on the pantograph or bow will spring off. Therefore, great care is needed and a degree of trial and error may need to be exercised.

The remainder of the overhead should be constructed in a similar way. This all sounds rather complicated but is really easier to do than to describe in writing. Where the overhead is to be used as a current supply it is not really practical to consider using it for electrical sectioning. It is far less of a problem to bond all the overheads together as one continuous supply and to use breaks in the track, as described in the previous chapter, to provide the sections. However, should it be necessary to use an overhead section, this is achieved by making a small joint from a piece of plastic with two small holes drilled into it as in Diagram 35. Then each end of the two sections of overhead is threaded through a different hole as the wire is bent over and cut to length. A similar device, but made of brass, can be used at the joints of portable baseboards. They should be soldered in place of the normal ear at the last traction hole on each part of the baseboard. A separate piece of wire is then used to join the overhead when the boards are placed together. It is better to use this type rather than just one joining strip because the part which gets most wear, the bend on the wire where it goes in and out of the joint, can easily break. Replacing the separate piece of wire is quite simple. If, however, it were a permanent part of the overhead a lot of work would be caused.

There are some model systems which are built purely for pantograph or bow use. On these layouts there is no need to use the same style of frogs at points. The wire departing from the main track can just be soldered alongside the main wire over the centre of the point. The sliding contact of the pantograph or bow does not need to be guided along the correct wire. It is necessary to ensure that the overhead support wires do not drop below the main overhead wire otherwise the pantograph could foul them bringing the tram to a sudden and unwanted

halt. This is why those trolley systems which did experiment with other types of collector did so with great care. Often complete routes had to be re-wired with suitable ears and hangers and there even had to be a complete re-aligning of the overhead wire. Those trams which were equipped with the new collecting device were then confined to just the modified route(s). Sometimes, more often in America, trams were equipped with both trolley and pantograph or bow, to enable them to run on any type of overhead. Indeed even one of the latest Boeing articulated trams in San Francisco has been equipped with a trolley pole at each end in addition to the single arm pantograph originally supplied.

At the terminus the tram with a pantograph needs no special treatment. The driver merely walks to the other end and is ready to drive away. In the case of the bow collector a little more care is required to ensure that the bow turns over, taking advantage of the slack in the overhead wire. This may be assisted by the conductor pulling on a rope attached to the bow. The situation is completely different for the tram with a trolley pole. This must be released from the wire, turned half a circle and re-located on the wire. In the days of the open-top tram this could be done by a competent conductor from the top deck. Although this had its hazards, as a novice conductor once discovered when the spring in the pole lifted him off his feet and the next thing he knew was that he found himself dangling from the trolley pole. With the onset of the covered tram there was no option but to walk around the car pulling the trolley pole into position. In later years, as the other traffic on the roads built up, it became evident that to walk in a large semi-circle around a tram looking up in the air was decidedly unsafe. To overcome this an arrangement of overhead wires and frogs was devised to do the job automatically and this was called the trolley reverser. This neat idea can be incorporated into the model layout and not only forms a very interesting visual effect but is also a very practical device. The photographs show the necessary arrangement and, as can be seen on the Picardy Tramways layout, the strength and stiffness of the model overhead reduces the amount of support wiring required.

Chapter 11

Depots

On a tramway the depot was the hub of activity. Small systems would usually have one depot which often contained the managers' offices as well as the repair and painting shops. The bulk of the depot was there to provide covered accommodation for the trams. But this was also the place where the drivers and conductors reported to take their trams out. Tickets were allocated and then checked by the finance staff against the conductors' takings. In some cases there were even people sorting and counting the little round pieces of ticket which were punched out by the ticket machine. All tickets of one price had a distinct colour and the day's takings could be checked exactly. Routine running repairs and minor accidental damage to the trams were undertaken by the specialist fitters and engineers. Those with extensive damage either went back to the manufacturers for rebuilding or were left in the back of the depot to be cannibalised for spares.

In the larger systems there would have been a main depot and repair shop which might even have undertaken tram construction or major rebuilding. This tradition has been, by necessity, carried forward to the present day where Blackpool Tramways are rebuilding some of their 1930s double-deck cars into the very modern Jubilee Class and The Seaton and District Tramways are building their own unique trams. Thus it is fitting that a model tramway layout should include a depot. By doing so the range and interest of operation will be very much increased. There is no need to follow the complexities of the larger operators. The depots of smaller systems provide a great deal of guidance for the small model. For example, the track layouts of the depots in the systems of Kidderminster and Stourport, and the Kinver Light Railway, are shown in Diagram 36. Each has its own individuality in a simple design which is easily modelled.

In the model form the overriding constraint is usually that of space. However, even on the smallest of layouts, a depot can be fitted. One example is shown in Diagram 37 where a board only 4 in wide still allows the construction of a small depot. The track construction is as described in Chapter Eight, but without the need to mark out setts inside the depot building. A cover of semi-matt black paint is sufficient for the built-up surface. If it is possible the inspection pits should be modelled. The pits should be marked out in the appropriate place, 16 mm wide. This strip of baseboard should be removed and some plywood fixed underneath to form the bottom of the pit. If commercial flexible track is used the sleeper strip should be removed and the rails supported by a suitable

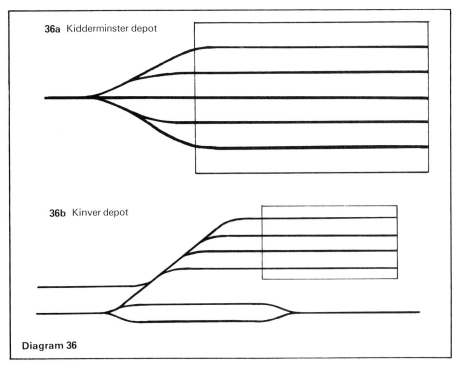

36a Kidderminster depot

36b Kinver depot

Diagram 36

Above Diagram 36: *Tram depots on small systems.*

Below *The sort of small depot which can be fitted into any layout to give extra interest to both operation and viewing* (model D. Sibley, photo D. Voice).

Above *A large model depot. Although full of continental trams the tram shed would be equally at home on a British layout. The traction poles on the track in the foreground are from the now defunct Hamo tramway system* (model and photo H. Gieramm).

Left *The two sheds to the left of the photo are constructed from pairs of Airfix model railway engine shed kits. That to the right is scratch-built* (model N. Dollimore, photo D. Voice).

Above right Diagram 37: *Layout for a model depot on a 4 in wide board (OO gauge).*

thickness of wood. The rails can be soldered to brass nails hammered in on the outside of them. The gauge of the track should be checked for trueness. A short staircase can be built from scrap wood and fitted in the end of the pit nearest the shed entrance. The other end can be left vertical. For real authenticity the sides of the pits should be covered with brick-embossed plastic card painted white to represent the ceramic bricks often found in such inspection pits.

To complete the picture a tram could be left on the pit in a state of repair. When a tram was in need of major maintenance or repair work the truck or bogies would be removed in a process akin to changing the wheels on a car. The body of the tram was raised a few inches by means of sturdy tram jacks. Two were used on each side. Once the tram had been raised, the truck or bogies were rolled out for electrical maintenance. The body was then usually lowered on to large baulks of timber. If a tram were modelled in this condition only the body need be made. It would provide an ideal opportunity to try out some of the techniques described in the first part of the book. Around the tram should be one or two figures suitably positioned to be working on the repairs.

The shed itself can be scratch-built or made up from engine shed kits such as

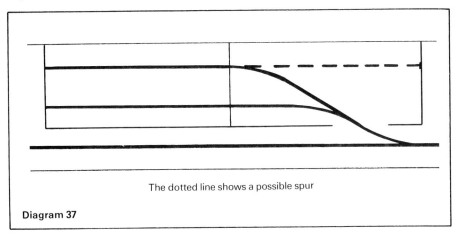

The dotted line shows a possible spur

Diagram 37

those producd by Airfix. Two or more mounted side by side produces a very authentic style tram shed, particularly if a few other buildings are also added. However, do ensure that either the roof is removable or that the whole building can be lifted away in order to reach any tram which may become stuck inside. Indeed, if you wish to go ahead with giving the tram shed real detail, you may wish to have the roof more or less permanently off in order that the inside of the building can be clearly seen. Naturally a fair bit of clutter should be scattered around the place. A few wheels on axles, resting near the back of the shed, workbenches along one side, odd bits of machinery, tram parts and jacks can be left around. A few crewmen clocking in or out could also be included.

To illustrate the features which can be incorporated I will use the tram works at Edge Lane, part of Liverpool Corporation Tramways, as an example (see Diagram 38). This purpose-built workshop was constructed in 1926 alongside an existing tram shed. This shed could house up to 60 trams and it occupied over an acre of ground. The workshops were on an even grander scale covering over seven acres with the administrative offices fronting Edge Lane itself. Running across the full width of the building, at its centre, was a traverser. This is a device which allows trams to be moved to any bay. It was used in preference to conventional pointwork because of the enormous saving in space it achieved. However, there was always the risk of a tram accidentally over-running a line when the traverser was not there and falling into the pit. This meant that all the trams on the side away from the traverser were stuck in the depot until the accident had been cleared. This was not too much of a problem in a works like Edge Lane, but in an operational depot it was a real headache especially if they were unlucky enough for it to happen just before the rush hour.

The working area was divided into a number of different specialised shops. The electrical shop looked after every part of the electrical equipment of the trams. Next came the car repair shop with its three overhead cranes and all the mechanical apparatus required for repair and construction work including wheel tyre heating machines and large lathes and grinding machines, all of which were used to retyre, machine and profile-grind the tram wheels. In a separate area was the blacksmith's shop with power hammers and shears, hearths and a case hardening oven, all to be used in connection with the iron framework of the tram. There was also a foundry for casting many of the parts

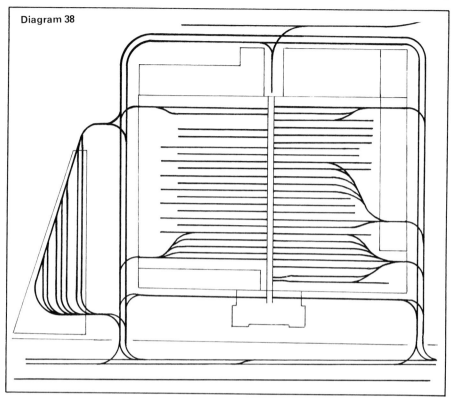

Diagram 38

for the trams and ancillary equipment in brass and aluminium. Next door was
the all-essential pattern shop.

Well cut off from the dust of the other shops was the paint shop which
included a sign writers gallery. In view of the need for cleanliness, it had its own
air conditioning system. Up to 40 trams could be in the shop at any one time.
Beyond the paint shop was the body repair shop and body building shop for
construction and major repair of tramcars. To keep these shops well supplied
there was a self-contained saw-mill leading to the cut timber store. Finally, there
was a well secured large store for the thousand and one parts needed in such a
repair works. Some indication of the activity in the building is the 109 ft of
counter in the stores, needed to keep the craftsmen supplied.

It is unlikely that you would have sufficient room to build a replica of this
depot and works on your layout. Indeed a model of the Edge Lane complex in
4 mm scale would require a space 12 ft × 13 ft. But you may like to incorporate
some of these features, albeit in a smaller proportion. The majority of tramway
systems would not have had such a comprehensive works and I would consider
that the foundry and pattern makers shops are less likely to be found. Although
some of the equipment used by them may be found in the smaller depots.
However, most depots did have a special paint shop. It was the usual practice to
give trams a repaint on a regular basis, sometimes as frequently as once a year in
order to preserve the bodywork and present a smart appearance to the public.
This was often a winter job when there was less demand on the service, freeing
both cars and men for the task. Often the paint shop would be no more than a

Depots

Left Diagram 38: *Edge Lane Depot and Workshops, Liverpool Corporation Tramways.*

Above right *Looking through the depot gates, this shot shows how effective the engine shed kits look when used in a depot* (model N. Dollimore, photo D. Voice).

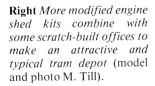

Right *More modified engine shed kits combine with some scratch-built offices to make an attractive and typical tram depot* (model and photo M. Till).

walled-off area capable of holding one or more cars. This was often achieved by bricking in the end of one bay of the shed and fitting large doors to give access to the rest of the depot. There would be plenty of light in the shop with glass let into the roof and being enhanced by painting the walls white.

Of, perhaps, more interest to the modeller is the idea of using the traverser as a feature of a depot. This may seem a major project but can be achieved without too many problems. The prototype often had as short a length as possible, even to the extent of being only slightly longer than the wheelbase of the tram. This meant that there was a large overhang at each end and the driver had to be very accurate when he stopped the tram on the traverser. In the model form it is easiest to eliminate electrical or mechanical stops by lining the tracks by eye. To do this it is necessary to make the traverser longer than the full length of the largest car. It also means that if your traverser is to be inside the shed the roof must be removable to enable you to see the operation. To make the traverser shown in Diagram 39, measure the longest car in your fleet (or that you plan to have) and add 1 in. This is the length that your traverser should be. A well must be cut in the baseboard to accommodate the moving platform and drive mechanism. The platform is made from plywood cut to the previously calculated length and some 2 in wide (for OO gauge). The track should be constructed on it by marking out the position of the rails an equal distance either side of the centre line. Hammer a few short brass nails just outside one of the lines, then solder the rail to the nailheads. Repeat for the other rail, this time checking that it is set at the correct gauge. A track gauge is useful but a steel rule

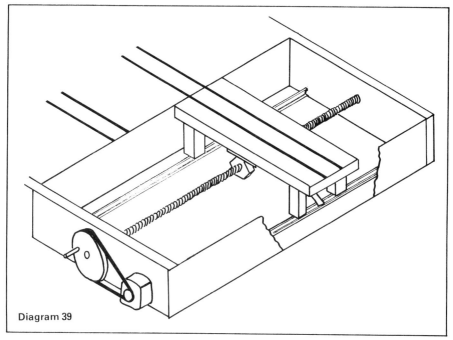

Diagram 39

Above Diagram 39: *Traverser for a model depot. See text for construction details.*
Below *Purley Depot on the London Transport system, after the closure of the system, showing the style of architecture and the inspection pits* (photo W.J. Haynes).

Below right *A London Transport traverser at Clapham Depot showing the overhang that was normal, but is not recommended when modelling these features. The tram is No 1779* (photo W.J. Haynes).

with ½ mm divisions can be used if your eyesight is good. For OO the gauge should be 16½ mm between the inside edges of the rail heads.

The rails must be cut to the same length as the platform and the inside edges of the rails chamfered slightly. The drive mechanism is a threaded rod of sufficient length to cover the full traverser operating distance as well as reaching the motor, which is best situated on the edge of the baseboard. The rod can be anything from $\frac{3}{16}$ in to $\frac{3}{8}$ in diameter depending on what you can find available. Thread two nuts on the rod and position them about 2 in apart (from their outer edges) and with a flat side uppermost. Clean off the oil or grease from these flats and tin them. Solder a piece of brass or tinplate 1 in × 2 in to them. Check that this plate runs smoothly up and down the thread as the rod is turned. At the ends of the traverser pit put a vertical mark at the centre and locate on it a point at a distance equal to that from the centre of the rod to the top of the plate plus the thickness of the plywood platform, minus the thickness of the sleepers, if you are using commercial railway track for the rest of the depot. This distance is measured from the top surface of the baseboard. Drill a clearance hole for the screwed rod. Repeat on the other end wall of the pit. Remove the plate and pass the rod through the holes replacing the plate in the pit. Fit a washer and two lock nuts on the non-powered end and a pulley wheel (if necessary held in place by two nuts) on the other end. Again check that all operates smoothly. It is rather crude to have the rod through a plain hole in the wood. If the traverser is likely to have a great deal of use the holes should be bushed with the appropriate size of metal tubing. Solder two lengths of rail to brass nails so that each runs along the bottom of the pit some ¼ in from the side walls. Lay the plywood platform over the metal plate and check that the top surface of the rails coincides with the top surface of the track to be used in the depot. If necessary sand down the underside of the plywood or put packing pieces between the plate and the platform.

When you are satisfied, measure the distance between the underside of the

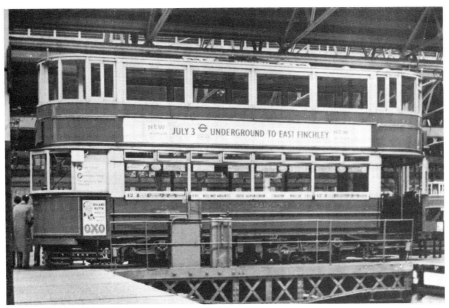

Left *Inside the depot on the Swansea and Mumbles Tramway. Note the inspection pits and the cat-walks to enable access to the upper deck exterior* (photo R.E. James-Robertson).

Above left *If this is not the most photographed depot in Britain I would be very surprised. It is of course the National Tramway Museum, Crich—an essential visiting place for all tramway modellers* (photo D. Voice).

Above *This photo is included not for the fine view of London Transport No 1597, but for the detail of Clapham Depot around it* (photo W.J. Haynes).

plywood and the top of the traverser pit rails. Cut four small pieces of wood to fit under the platform and rest on the rails. Hammer two brass nails beneath the platform to go right through the plywood. They should be on the centre line and about 1 in to 1½ in from the middle. A strip of nickel silver or phosphor bronze is soldered to the nail so that it will rub along one rail when the platform is in position. Repeat for the other side. The upper part of the nails should be cut flush and each connected to one running rail by thin wire. This will provide the electrical feed to the running rails via the rails in the traverser pit. The platform can now be fixed to the plate by either directly gluing with contact adhesive or using small nuts and bolts to allow removal for any subsequent repair work.

The drive motor should be of the 12-volt dc type and mounted on a bracket on the side of the baseboard. A small pulley should be attached to the shaft and connected by means of a rubber band, or better still, a spring drive band, to the other pulley. The motor should be connected to the controller through a double pole double throw switch. This will ensure that the power to the track is isolated when the traverser is in operation and vice versa. The use of the controller makes the job of lining the tracks up by eye much more simple as the final adjustment can be done at slow speed while the long movements can be carried out at higher speeds. Check that all runs smoothly and set the traverser at the places where the other tracks are to join it. These tracks can now be laid ensuring that the rails on either side of the traverser pit line up with those on the traverser. The rail edges should be chamfered to allow a small degree of latitude when lining up. When all is satisfactory the floor of the depot can be built up, the traverser pit and traverser painted and all necessary details such as handrails can be added.

Finally, the model depot can be completed with some of the many specialised vehicles used by the works and maintenance staff. Most obvious of these is the overhead repair wagon. These road vehicles were often converted lorries or even buses at the end of their working life, which had towers added to enable the maintenance workers to reach the overhead wiring. The more modern type of vehicle is usually purpose-built and has hydraulically-operated arms to lift a working platform to the desired position. Where the tramway system incorporated reserved track with a railway type sleeper construction the road vehicles are unable to gain access to these areas. So the systems have specially converted works trams with towers. Naturally when the overhead is being repaired it must be switched off and so such vehicles have generators built into them to enable them to move under their own power, or they can use the overhead power when it is available. There would also often be a number of works trailers for a variety of other purposes, which all make delightful subjects to model.

Chapter 12

Scenery

To my mind there is only one proper place for a model tram and that is running in its appropriate setting. For the historical British tram model this usually means an urban environment. Apart from a minority of country routes like the Burton and Ashby, Kinver Light Railway and Swansea and Mumbles—and also the occasional reserved track found in the city systems—the British tram was essentially a town vehicle. Indeed in the heyday of the tram between the Wars, the most conspicuous aspect of most photographs of the period is the absence of other forms of transport. The occasional horse-drawn vehicle and hand cart were sometimes seen and, consistently, the back drop to this scene was rows of houses and shops, with occasional industrial areas. Usually there was at least one football ground with its tram sidings full of empty 'specials' waiting for the crowds to come out at the end of the game. This was, and still is, the special quality of the tram as a public service vehicle. It has no equal at moving large numbers of people over relatively short distances.

One aspect of the scenic side which has always appealed to me is researching those houses and shops which will fit the scene I am aiming to create. I have some particularly favourite parts of my home town which have the most delightful Victorian housing and corner shops. The simplest way of recording the buildings is to take photographs. For terraced property a few shots of the front are usually sufficient, but where there are single houses or corner shops I try to get as many sides as I can without trespassing. However, many owners seem to be flattered when asked if photos can be taken and usually are willing to allow you to go through on to their private property. When modelling such buildings my aim is to create the general impression and atmosphere of a given house rather than to try and create a perfect miniature of it. Therefore, I am not averse to mixing parts from different buildings in order to create the precise style I am seeking. If your choice is to create in miniature an actual street from a town you may well have to search for early photographs of the buildings in order to be able to build an exact replica.

Again, if your desire is to create a precise period then you will want to have an idea of the age of the buildings which you are considering. Sometimes there are stones built into the house or row of terraced cottages giving the date of construction and, perhaps, the name of that little development. Some produce a wry smile now with names like Meadow Cottages and Pleasant View in rather run-down industrial areas of a town. You will find that after a while you will be able roughly to date any building by its location and style. Although there are

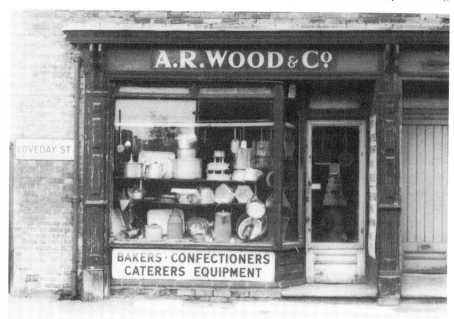

Above *Whilst researching this book I took a wrong turning in the centre of Birmingham and came across this shop. It is ideal for a period tramway layout as it looks as if it has not changed since the day it opened* (photo D. Voice).

Above right *The background of the Bispham to Little Bispham layout consists of enlargements of photographs of the actual buildings along the Blackpool Tramway. Not only is it entirely authentic, it also needs no space* (model A. Kirkman, photo D. Voice).

Below *Very low relief shops forming the background to Tamebridge Tramways. These are scratch-built models based on actual shops in the home area of the modeller* (model and photo M. Till).

often single houses very much out of period with the rest of a street. With terraced cottages there are some noticeable changes in style. The earliest Victorian rows had a door with a single window upstairs and downstairs. Later the interior layout changed and a window appeared above the front door, then later still there were bay windows downstairs. Early houses tend to have no front gardens, later ones may well have a small front area bounded by a low brick wall. However, it is not possible to be exact because these changes were the result of evolution rather than abrupt moves from one style to another. However, you may get the feeling for the general sort of period in your own town. Dating can also be helped by calling in at your local library and looking through the historic maps in the reference section. The larger scale maps will show individual buildings and by comparing one map with another the developments carried out between survey dates can easily be seen. This can be related to actual exploration of the streets. Here again the value of photographs is shown, as the sort of area which interests the modeller is often at risk from the developer's bulldozer.

Rather than draw the building and then construct the model I prefer to work directly from the photograph. This is quite easy to do if you use brick-embossed plastic card or printed brick paper and the type of building you are modelling is brick faced. Firstly check that the brick pattern of the paper or plastic card is similar to that of the building. For older constructions the brick bond will be 'English', which looks like alternating full bricks and half-bricks. The later style used in cavity walls was 'Flemish' bond which has no half-brick sizes. If you cannot get a proper match it is still possible to use this direct method but a little more care needs to be taken in horizontal measurements. The next thing to do is check whether the brick sheet has been made to OO or HO scale. In OO there are approximately 22 rows of brick to each 1 in height, whilst in HO it is approximately 26 rows. Using a clear photograph it is simple to determine

A row of half depth shops on the Wolverhampton Corporation layout. Again a nice eye for detail (model K. Thompson, photo D. Voice).

heights and lengths of the building and window and door spacings in numbers of bricks. These can be directly counted on the model brick material using a brick-for-brick measure if the scale is correct. However, if you are modelling in OO and the material you are using has been made in HO scale (and it is worth noting that all the embossed plastic card sheets which I have come across have been HO) you must add one brick to every seven in the photograph. That is for each measurement in bricks on the photo the number must be multiplied by 8 over 7 before transferring to the modelling sheet. This applies to both horizontal and vertical measurements. In this way a complete building can be made without once using a rule.

To create the illusion of a town street while using little layout space the time-honoured modelling method is to use low-relief buildings as the back scene. In front of them the pavement and street are modelled complete with tram tracks and overhead wiring. The method to use the least space possible is to put the scenery on a flat sheet of plywood. The street houses and the rest of the town are pictured in two dimensions on the back scene. Indeed, there is a scenic paper produced specifically for this purpose called 'Town-Scene'. The plywood screen should be covered with sky paper, there are a number of different types available but all show blue sky with various cloud formations. The background part of the scenic paper is then carefully cut out and pasted to the sky paper, using cellulose wallpaper paste. Finally the foreground houses are cut and glued in whatever sequence is desired. The more artistic can produce the same effect, but on an individual basis, by painting the required area on the plywood. Alternatively, where the model depicts a real section of prototype system, photos can be taken of the actual buildings and by having appropriate enlargements made an absolutely correct background can be formed. I have seen all three methods successfully used on layouts. The major advantages are the simplicity of construction, the consequent saving of time over building rows of model houses and, of course, the saving in space. Using this technique a complete street scene with double tram track can be built in OO gauge on a shelf just 4 in wide. There are disadvantages—no matter how realistic the images seem, they are still flat. There is no three dimensional feel about them.

This can be countered to good effect by using the low-relief method. Here the impression of a full building is created using the depth of 1 in or less. There are various levels at which this can be done. The most simple is to use the 'Town-Scene' sheets and mount the foreground buildings on stiff card, if necessary, with extra bracing. The roofs should be bent over to the appropriate angle and the chimneys pushed back to the vertical position, where necessary cutting into the roof to the base of the chimney stack. Using spare brick print from parts of the sheet not already used, make up the sides of the chimney stacks and the sides of any buildings where the roof height changes from one to another. The chimneys should be completed by a square of card being placed on top and the chimney-pots themselves then being added. I find the simplest and most effective method of making chimney pots is to use children's drinking straws.

A three-quarter depth bike shop with the products spilling on to the pavement (model D. Watkins, photo D. Voice).

More three-quarters depth buildings. This time the pub on the Wolverhampton Corporation layout. Note the period figures waiting at the tram stop (model K. Thompson, photo D. Voice).

These are cut to length and painted brick red on the outside. After gluing them into place the inner surface is given a coat of matt black. The finished item is most realistic. For variety, the lengths of the pots should not all be the same. I use about three main lengths and choose the middle one for most of the chimney pots but give a fair sprinkling of the others to give a good visual impact. This method of low-relief building is very quick and the three-dimensional effect of the roofs does deceive the eye and the fact that the rest of the building is quite flat (even to the extent of retaining the printed windows) is not noticeable.

The next stage is to build low-relief models which incorporate features on the surface such as recessed windows, window sills, bay windows, columns in the brickwork and other such projections. The techniques used in this type of building are well known and can be found in the *PSL Model Railway Guide No 3, Structure Modelling*, by Michael Andress, so I will not go into them here except to say that even the smallest amount of building up on a flat surface can make an enormous difference to the impact of the model on the scene.

There are a number of appropriate scale kits available in cardboard or plastic which produce very nice buildings. Some of the card kits are specifically low-relief, giving a realistic impression of a solid structure yet only needing ½ in in depth. The full building kits can also be used by cutting along half the depth and, of course, the rear can also be used as another building giving two for the price of one. With the cardboard kits it is very simple to apply your own modifications, to mix parts from different kits and generally change the buildings. This not only allows you to fit the precise requirements of your layout but also enables you to put your own character into them. The finished model is then very much yours, rather than being identifiable as a row of standard kits.

Full buildings forming the bulk of the town complex of Tamebridge Tramways. The added interest of having trams appearing and disappearing behind buildings is well illustrated in this photo (model and photo M. Till).

This now leads into the construction of complete buildings. Although there is no rule in the matter, I consider that the term low-relief really ends when the model represents more than half the depth of the building.

For producing complete buildings there is a choice between either scratch-building or using kits. Perhaps this is a suitable point to pass on some of my own lessons. The first buildings which I constructed were made from cardboard covered with brick-paper. Later on the brick embossed plastic card was introduced and I felt that the extra texture provided by the moulding was excellent. A number of buildings were made from this material. The brick surface was painted in appropriate colours of matt enamel. When this had hardened the building was given a weathered look by over-painting with thin water colours. The first coat was applied with an old toothbrush and I scrubbed the enamel surface until the water colour took to it. The muted colours—coupled with the ability to wipe off excess and add a whole variety of shades—produce a very satisfactory finish. However, there were two mistakes which I made. I used a solvent glue and just one thickness of plastic card. The result is that the buildings have warped and twisted. It really is necessary to provide a firm base for the plastic card. Indeed, I am now inclined to use the embossed card only for effect and I do not try to add strength to the structure with it. In addition the manufacturers have been developing some delightful ranges of brick-papers with subtle colour variations and true scale bricks. I have seen very realistic models made using these papers and there now seems to be little to choose between the paper and plastic for realism. Certainly I have had less problems with the traditional card and paper constructions. However, it does seem to be a matter for personal choice as many modellers I have met are

completely satisfied with both mediums. Plastic kits use a different type of material which is moulded with a thick enough section not to require extra support and which resists warping.

This chapter, so far, has concentrated on individual buildings. However, the great art of scenic modelling is the overall balance of the whole setting. What the modeller is trying to achieve is an atmosphere of the real thing. It is hard to describe what is meant by the word 'atmosphere' in regard to models. In a sense it is the capacity of a model to evoke a response in the viewer in identifying with the scene. The difficulty is that an exact scale replica of an object may have no atmosphere at all and yet an out-of-scale or freehand model may be full of it. Atmosphere is a most elusive quality and, in a way, the scenic modeller must be like an artist composing a painting. However, while the artist works on a flat canvas the modeller is working in three dimensions. Just as a painting with a dominant feature is easier to compose so a scene with a special feature is less of a problem in modelling. Although the tramway itself is usually the prominent feature it is useful to include some other eye-catching constructions. They may be large or small and should be connected with other features. Many such can be seen in the photos in this second section of the book, but it is worth while to draw attention to some of them. The larger items include tramway depots, large factories, a town's ancient gateway and a large canal basin complete with warehouses and long boats. At the other end of the spectrum are the gang digging a hole in the road, window cleaners at work, or revellers enjoying themselves in the town square.

One example of the inter-linking of small features to present a complete picture and create the desired atmosphere is Picardy Tramways. At the one end there is the tram terminus, trolley reverser and pub. A little further up the street the tramway moves into the background and a park with bandstand and fishpond take the eye with some highly detailed shops forming the back-drop. Then the clock tower leads the eye to the market scene contained in the turning loop and, at the end of the layout is the church. It is this setting of small scenes within the overall picture which, for me, creates the interest giving the layout enough character to be worth a long lingering look even when the trams are no longer running. One of the great contributions to this feeling is the use of people in the scene. With the range of model figures now available there is no problem

Above left *The sort of scene that gives interest to a layout. Here a gang works on the track under the watchful eye of the foreman* (model A. Kirkman, photo D. Voice).

Above *Another gang works on the road, while a lady in the background buys flowers from a costermonger* (model K. Thompson, photo D. Voice).

Right *A street market should always be a hive of activity and the Picardy market is no exception* (model D. Watkins, photo D. Voice).

in populating your town. Although the number of non-military figures is limited, it is very simple to use the miniature soldiers and by carving with a craft knife and adding a few bits of Milliput they can be turned into civilians. Painting them can be a chore but with practice the job can be carried out quite quickly. I used to apply each colour on separate evenings and allowed the paint to dry fully each time. After use I carefully washed out the fine (00) brush. Now, after the practice I have had, I use a much larger brush (3) and have all the colours around me moving from figure to figure and colour to colour as I go. The brush is squeezed out on a tissue handkerchief between different colours.

I always mount my figures on pins which are then glued into holes drilled in the baseboard. For plastic figures the pin is heated red hot over the gas stove and pushed up a leg. The first few which I did lost a leg in the process, but I soon got the hang of it and I even used some of the early 'wooden leg' models on a layout. On white metal figures the pin is soldered to the outside of the leg

furthest from the viewing side. Once the pin is attached to the figure it can be used as a handle during painting. Rows of figures waiting for the paint to dry can be poked into a block of Plasticine. They can be taken out one at a time for further details to be painted as the appropriate paint tin is opened. The main method used is to paint the major colour all over the model. Since matt colours are used throughout they dry fairly quickly and, if a couple of dozen figures are dealt with at a time, when the last one is painted the first is dry enough for further colours. Details like hair, coats, scarves, shoes, and even in some cases shirts and ties, are picked out in the appropriate colour. The final touch is some flesh colour to the face, hands and, for the ladies, the legs. If the paint brush does slip and paint gets where it should not be, then I just leave it all to dry and then over-paint with the appropriate colour. The average figure has four colours and a couple of dozen can be painted in an evening.

If your layout includes some countryside, then the same techniques as those used by railway modellers can be put to good effect. Where there is reserved track it is easier to use one of the ready-made flexible tracks fixed to the baseboard with thin pins. I find that the simplest method of laying ballast is to pour it over the track and, using a paint brush, level it off with the sleepers and form the edges of the ballasted area. Then, using an eye dropper, drip some watered-down white glue, as used in woodwork, over it all. The glue should be diluted with water in the ratio one part glue to two parts water. When it dries there will be no sign of the glue on the ballast but it will be held firmly in place. There is another advantage in using this water-based white glue; it can be removed by applying hot water. So if you need to re-lay any track a kettle of hot water will shift the ballast and allow it to be re-aligned. The same glue can be used to fix into place other scenic scatter material such as grass or gravel. Trees and bushes can be added using either dyed lichen or one of the tree kits now available. All these items, and also advice on scenic modelling, can be had from your local model railway shop.

Once you have built your layout the best way of checking it is to take a few photographs. These will highlight any areas which need attention. It is also useful to try out a number of different camera angles with your favourite tram models.

Above left *Despite the North London steam tram, this is a continental narrow gauge tramway. Again it is brought to life with the expert use of a market place. This and the other photos in the book should provide plenty of ideas for enlivening your layout* (model D. Sibley, photo D. Voice).

Left *I always thought it was impossible for one tiny OO gauge figure to create an aura of atmosphere until I was introduced to this Black Country fellow with his whippet* (model K. Thompson, photo D. Voice).

Illustrated glossary

For those unfamiliar with tram terminology the following annotated diagrams should provide a useful guide. The three main tram varieties are described in detail and their various parts are picked out on each drawing.

Open-top tram

Trolley head

Trolley pole

Ventilators

Trolley standard

Canopy bend

Decency boards

Cant rail

Canopy

Quarterlights

Handbrake

Vent rail

Dash

Grab rail

Solebar or sill

Truck

Lifeguard tray or drop tray

Bulkhead

Step

DON THOMAS

Balcony tram

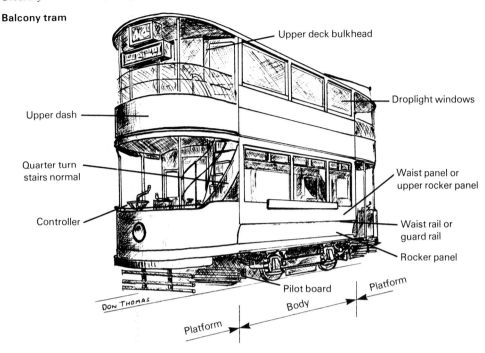

Upper deck bulkhead

Droplight windows

Upper dash

Quarter turn
stairs normal

Controller

Waist panel or
upper rocker panel

Waist rail or
guard rail

Rocker panel

DON THOMAS

Pilot board

Platform

Body

Platform

Platform

Enclosed tram

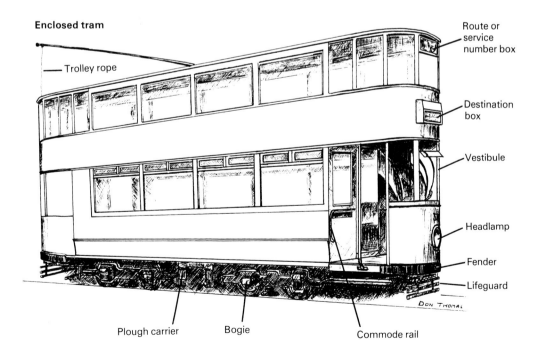

Route or
service
number box

Trolley rope

Destination
box

Vestibule

Headlamp

Fender

Lifeguard

DON THOMAS

Plough carrier

Bogie

Commode rail

Appendix 1

Kits for British electric tramway systems

Introduction

This list does not claim to be exhaustive but will give the prospective modeller a guide to the availability of kits for a favourite town or system. All the kits listed can be constructed with little or no modification to represent one or more types of car run on the system chosen. However, the kits may not have the precise wheelbase or truck design.

It is quite possible that other kits can be modified to suit other types of tram. These will require the more advanced modelling techniques described in this book.

In all cases it is recommended that a photo of the desired type of tram is used and that some research is carried out to determine the appropriate colours and style of livery.

Key
Bec Kits

These are noted in the list by number taken from the 1981 catalogue. The letter after the number denotes either Direct (D) or Reversed (R) stairs. It is important to get this prominent feature correct. If the kit bought does not have the type of stairs required the appropriate parts can be purchased as spares direct from Bec

This is Blackpool No 8, one of the rebuilt 1930s trams to form the OMO series. It marks a new era in the life of the tramway (photo D. Voice).

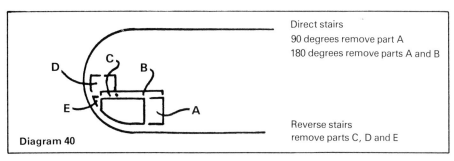

Direct stairs
90 degrees remove part A
180 degrees remove parts A and B

Reverse stairs
remove parts C, D and E

Diagram 40

Kits. The floor of these kits can be made to take either type of stair and the appropriate modifications are as shown above.

Anbrico
AB	=	Bradford Balcony
AS	=	Sheffield Roberts

The new range of Anbrico kits is identified by the manufacturer's catalogue number and consists of two letters followed by two numbers. For example BT43 means the balcony top car with four windows in the upper deck saloon and three in the lower saloon.

Model Tramcar Design
MTDR	=	Blackpool Toast-rack
MTDP	=	Blackpool Pantograph Car
MTDS	=	Blackpool Standard

Bournemouth Passenger Transport Association
BPTA	=	Bournemouth No 60 (ex-Poole No 6)

Varney Transport Replicas
VGG(L)	=	Liverpool Green Goddess
VGG(G)	=	Glasgow Green Goddess
VSD	=	Southampton Dome
VSD(L)	=	Leeds car ex-Southampton Dome
VHR	=	London County Council HR2

K's (Keyser)
KE	=	Metropolitan Electric Tramways Type E

System	Gauge ft in	Kits	Notes
Aberdare UDC Tramways	3 6	3D, OT30	
Aberdeen Corporation Tramways	4 8½	8D, 9D, BT44, CT44	
Aberdeen Suburban Tramways Co Ltd	4 8½		
Accrington Corporation Tramways	4 0	BT43, CT44, OT30	Headlights on upper dash. Remove quarterlights from BT43.

System	Gauge ft in	Kits	Notes
Airdrie and Coatbridge Tramways Co	4 7¾	8D, 9D	
Ashton-Under-Lyne Corporation Tramways	4 8½	3D, 4D	
Ayr Corporation Tramways	4 8½	3D, 9D	
Barking Town UDC Light Railways	4 8½	3R, 4D	
Barnsley and District Electric Traction Co Ltd	4 8½	3R	
Barrow-in-Furness Corporation Tramways	4 0	3D, 8D	
Bath Electric Tramways Ltd	4 8½	3D	
Batley Corporation Tramways	4 8½	3R	
Belfast Corporation Tramways	4 8½	3D, CT44	
Bessbrook and Newry Tramways	3 0		
Bexley Heath UDC Tramways	4 8½	2D	Ex-LCC purchased 1917
Birkenhead Corporation Tramways	4 8½	3D	
Birmingham Corporation Tramways	3 6	3D, 4D, 9D, 12 BT33, BT44	Kit 12 will need slight modifications to suit
Birmingham and Midland Tramways Joint Committee	3 6	3D, 5, 8D, 9D BT44	Remove upper deck quarterlights on BT44
Birmingham District Power and Traction Co Ltd	3 6	3D, 5, 8D, 9D BT44	Remove upper deck quarterlights from BT44
Blackburn Corporation Tramways	4 0		
Blackpool Corporation Tramways	4 8½	3R, MTDR, MTDP, MTDS	3R remove upper deck floor above stairs
Bolton Corporation Tramways	4 8½	11D	
Bournemouth Corporation Tramways	3 6	3D, 5, BPTA	Cover quarterlights and make top of windows into tudor arch
Bradford City Tramways	4 0	11R, AB	
Brighton Corporation Tramways	3 6	3D, 3R, OT30	Headlamp on top deck end decency panels. OT30 needs hex dash modification

System	Gauge ft in	Kits	Notes
Brighton and Rottingdean Seashore Railway	Two tracks 2 8½ gauge set 18 ft apart		
Bristol Tramways & Carriage Co	4 8½	5, also 5 with 4 window sides	Cover quarterlights and make top of windows into tudor arch
Burnley Corporation Tramways	4 0		
Burton & Ashby Light Railway	3 6	3D	
Burton Upon Trent Corporation Tramways	3 6	3R, 4R, OT30	
Bury Corporation Tramways	4 8½	3D, CT43	
Cambourne & Redruth Light Railway	3 6	3R	
Cardiff Corporation Tramways	4 8½	5, CT44, OT40	Remove quarterlights from upper deck of CT44
Chatham and District Light Railways	3 6	3D, 8D, 8R	Headlights on upper dash
Cheltenham & District Light Railway	3 6	3R, 8R*, OT30, OT40	8 needs the small upright in middle of each quarterlight removed
Chester Corporation Tramways	3 6	5	Replace 3 window side with 4 window spare bought separately
Chesterfield Corporation Tramways	4 8½	8D, 9D	
City of Birmingham Tramways	3 6	8D, 9D, BT33, BT44	
City of Carlisle Tramways Co Ltd	3 6	3D	
Colchester Corporation Tramways	3 6	3R	
Colne Corporation Light Railways	4 0	3D	
Cork Electric Tramway	2 11½	8D	Headlights to upper dash. Cover quarterlights
Coventry Corporation Tramways	3 6	3D, 3R, BT33	
Croydon Corporation Tramways	4 8½	3D, 3R, 12	
Cruden Bay Electric Tramways	3 6		

System	Gauge ft in	Kits	Notes
Darlington Corporation Light Railways	3 6	4D, BT33	Vestibules required
Dartford UDC Light Railway	4 8½	3D	
Darwen Corporation Tramways	4 0	OT30	
Dearne and District Light Railway Joint Committee	4 8½		
Derby Corporation Tramways	4 0	3D, 11D	
Devonport & District Tramways Co	3 6	3D, 5	Windows need to be modified to tudor arch. Very low upper deck decency panels
Dewsbury Corporation Tramways	4 8½	3D	
Dewsbury, Ossett and Soothill Nether Tramways	4 8½	4D	
Doncaster Corporation Tramways	4 8½	3R, 4D, 9D, BT44	Remove quarterlights from upper deck of BT44
Douglas Head Marine Drive Ltd	4 8½		
Dover Corporation Tramways	3 6	3D, 3R, 4D, 9D, OT40, BT33	Headlights on upper dash trolley pole side mounted
Dublin United Tramways Co	5 3	3R, OT40, BT44	
Dudley Corporation Tramways	3 6	3D, 8D, 9D	
Dudley, Stourbridge and District Electric Traction Co Ltd	3 6	3D, 5, 8D, 9D OT40, BT44	Remove part of vestibules and top deck quarter-lights from OT40 and BT44
Dumbarton, Burgh and County Tramways Co Ltd	4 7¾	9D	
Dundee, Broughty Ferry and District Tramways Co Ltd	4 8½	5	
Dundee Corporation	4 8½	5, CT44	
Dunfermline and District Tramways Co	3 6	8D	
East Ham Corporation Tramways	4 8½	3R, 4D, 12	

System	Gauge ft in	Kits	Notes
Edinburgh Corporation Tramways	4 8½	4D, 9D, 11D, BT44, CT43, CT44, OT30	4D through car from Musselborough
Erith UDC Tramways	4 8½	8D, 9D	
Exeter Corporation Tramways	3 6	3D, OT30	
Falkirk and Districk Tramways Co	4 0	3D, 4D	
Farnworth UDC Tramways	4 8½	8R	
Gateshead & District Tramways Co	4 8½	3R, 6D, BT44, CT33, CT44	
Giants Causeway Tramway	3 0		
Glasgow Corporation Tramways	4 7¾	3D, 15, VGG(G)	
Glossop UDC Tramways	4 8½	3R	
Gloucester Corporation Light Railways	3 6	8D, OT40	Remove part of vestibule on OT40
Gosport and Fairham Tramways	4 7¾	3D	Headlights on upper dash
Gravesend and Northfleet Electric Tramways Ltd	4 8½	3D, 8R	
Great Crosby Tramways (Liverpool Overhead Rly)	4 8½	3R, 4D, 5	
Great Grimsby Street Tramways	4 8½	2R, 3R	Headlights on upper dash
Great Yarmouth Corporation Tramways	3 6	8D, 8R	
Greenock and Port Glasgow Tramways Co	4 7¾	8D	
Grimsby Corporation Tramways	4 8½	11R	
Grimsby and Immingham Electric Railway	4 8½		
Guernsey Tramway Co Ltd	4 8½	5	One end of the model will need modifying as both entrances were on the same side
Halifax Corporation Tramways	3 6	8D, BT44, OT40	
Hamilton, Motherwell and Wishaw Light Railways Co Ltd	4 7¾	3R	Headlights on upper dash
Hampshire Light Railways (Electric) Ltd	4 7¾	3R	

System	Gauge	Kits	Notes
	ft in		
Hartlepools Electric Tramways	3 6	5	
Hastings Tramways Co	3 6	3D	Headlights should be on upper deck end decency panels
Hill of Howth Tramways	5 3		
Huddersfield Corporation Tramways	4 7¾	3R, 5, BT44, CT44	
City of Hull Tramways	4 8½	3R, 9D	Headlights to upper dash, 9D only vestibuled
Ilford UDC Tramway	4 8½	2D, 3R, 4D	3R cover quarterlights and give tudor arches to windows
Ilkeston Corporation Tramways	3 6	3R	
Ipswich Corporation Tramways	3 6	3R	
Isle of Thanet Electric Tramways and Lighting Co Ltd	3 6	8R, OT40	Headlights on upper dash. Also covers Broadstairs, Margate, Ramsgate
Jarrow & District Electric Traction Co Ltd	4 8½	3R, 6D	
Keighley Corporation Tramways	4 0	3D, 4D, 11	
Kidderminster & Stourport Electric Tramways	3 6	8D	
Kilmarnock Corporation Tramways	4 8½	3D	
Kinver Light Railway	3 6		
Kirkcaldy Corporation	3 6	3D, 3R	
Lanarkshire Tramways Co	4 7¾	3D, 3R, OT30, BT44	Headlights on upper dash
Lancaster Corporation Tramways	4 8½	8D, 8R	Headlights on upper dash
Leamington & Warwick Electric Co Ltd	3 6	8D	
Leeds City Tramways	4 8½	3R, 5, 10, 11, VSD(L), BT44, CT33, CT44	
Leicester Corporation Tramways	4 8½	2R, 3R, 4R	Roof needs building up to semi-dome profile, use plastic padding or similar
Leith Corporation Tramways	4 8½	3D, 8D, 9D	
Leyton Corporation Tramways	4 8½	3D, 4D, 12	12 will need modification into E/3

System	Gauge ft in	Kits	Notes
City of Lincoln Tramways	4 8½	3D, 4D	
Liverpool Corporation Tramways	4 8½	3R, 5, VGG(L), CT43	
Llandudno and Colwyn Bay Electric Railway Ltd	3 6		MTDR could pass as the toast-rack but the seating is not correct
Llanelly & District Electric Lighting & Traction Co Ltd	4 8½	8D	
London County Council Tramways	4 8½	2D, 2R, 3R, 4R, 12, VHR	
London United Tramways Ltd	4 8½	14	
Lowestoft Corporation Tramways	3 6	8R	Cover quarterlights and make top of windows into tudor arch
Luton Corporation Tramways	4 8½	3D	
Lytham St Annes Tramways	4 8½	3R	Headlights on upper dash
Maidstone Corporation Tramways	3 6	3D	
Manchester Corporation Tramways	4 8½	3D, 3R	3D through car from Stockport, 3R from Salford
Mansfield & District Light Railways	4 8½	4D, 8D	
Manx Electric Railway Co Ltd	3 0		
Merthyr Electric Traction & Lighting Co Ltd	3 6	3D, 8D, OT30, OT40	
Metropolitan Electric Tramways Co Ltd	4 8½	14, KE	
Mexborough and Swinton Traction Co	4 8½	3D, 4D	
Middlesborough, Stockton & Thornaby Electric Tramways (Imperial Tramways Co Ltd)	3 7	None	
Middleton Electric Traction Co Ltd	4 8½	3D	
Musselburgh and District Electric Light and Traction Co Ltd	4 8½	3R, 4D	
Nelson Corporation Tramways	4 0	4D	
Newcastle Corporation Tramways	4 8½	8R, BT44	

System	Gauge	Kits	Notes
	ft in		
Newport (Mon) Corporation Tramways	4 8½	2D, 3D, 3R, CT33	Kit 3 needs headlight on upper deck end decency panels. Kit 2 type purchased from LCC.
Northampton Corporation Tramways	3 6	3R	
Norwich Electric Tramways Co	3 6	8D	Remove upper deck floor over platforms
Nottingham Corporation Tramways	4 8½	3R, 4D, 4R, BT43, BT44	Remove quarterlights from upper deck windows on BT44
Nottingham & Derbyshire Tramways Co	4 8½	8D, 9D	
Oldham Corporation Tramways	4 8½	4D	
Ossett Corporation Tramways	4 8½	3D	
Paisley and District Tramways Co	4 7¾	3D	
Perth Corporation Tramways	3 6	3D	
Peterborough Electric Traction Co Ltd	3 6	3R, 8D	
Plymouth Corporation Tramways	3 6	3D, 8D, OT30	
Plymouth, Stonehouse & Devonport Tramways Co	3 6	3R, 3D	
Pontypridd UDC Tramways	3 6	8D	8D later fitted with Bellamy type top cover
Poole Corporation Tramways	3 6	5, BPTA	
Portsdown and Horndean Light Railway	4 7¾	3R	Headlight on upper dash
Portsmouth Corporation Tramways	4 7¾	3R, CT33, OT30	Remove upper deck quarterlights from CT33
Potteries Electric Traction Co	4 0		
Preston Corporation Tramways	4 8½	5	Tudor arch at top of windows
Rawtenstall Corporation Tramways	4 0	3D, 4D	
Reading Corporation Tramways	4 0	3R, 8D, OT40	
Rhondda Tramways Co Ltd	3 6	3D	
Rochdale Corporation Tramways	4 8½	3D, CT33	

System	Gauge ft in	Kits	Notes
Rochester Corporation Tramways	3 6	8R	Headlights on upper dash
Rotherham Corporation Tramways	4 8½	2D, 3R, 4D CT44B	2D is ex-LCC, purchased 1917
Rothesay Tramways Co Ltd	3 6	MTDR	
St Helen's Corporation Tramways	4 8½	BT33	Add upper deck quarter-lights
Salford Corporation Tramways	4 8½	3R, CT44B, OT30	
Scarborough Tramways Co	3 6	3D, 3R	
Seaton and District Tramway Co	2 9		
Sheerness and District Electric Power and Traction Co Ltd	3 6	8R	Replace trolley pole with large bow collectors mounted on normal standard
Sheffield City Tramways	4 8½	2D, 9D, AS, CT44	2D is ex-LCC, purchased 1917 CT44 should be modified to hex dash
Snaefell Mountain Railway	3 6		
Soothill Nether Urban District Tramways	4 8½	3D	
Southampton Corporation Tramways	4 8½	2D, 3D, 4D, VSD, TT50	2D is ex-LCC purchased 1918
Southend-on-Sea Corporation Tramways	3 6	3D	
South Lancashire Tramways	4 8½	3D, 3R	Headlights on upper dash
South Metropolitan Electric Tramways & Lighting Co	4 8½	3D, 8D	
Southport Corporation Tramways	4 8½	3R, TT50	
South Shields Corporation Tramways	4 8½	8D, CT44B	
South Staffs Tramways (Lessee) Co Ltd	3 6	3R, 5, 8D, 11R	
Stalybridge, Hyde, Mossley and Dunkinfield Joint Tramways and Electric Board	4 8½	3D, 5	
Stockport Corporation Tramways	4 8½	3D, 3R, CT33, CT44	
Stockton and Thornaby Joint Corporation Tramways	3 7		

System	Gauge ft in	Kits	Notes
Sunderland Corporation Tramways	4 8½	3R, CT33, CT44, OT30	Remove upper deck quarterlights from CT33
Sunderland District Electric Tramways Ltd	4 8½	3D	
Swansea Improvements & Tramways Co Ltd	4 8½	8D	
Swansea and Mumbles Railway	4 8½		
Swindon Corporation Tramways	3 6	3D, 3R	
Taunton Electric Traction Co Ltd	3 6	8R	Headlight on upper dash and tudor arch windows
Torquay Tramways Co Ltd	3 6	3D	Originally surface contact therefore no trolley pole. Overhead system fitted 1911
Tynemouth & District Electric Traction Co Ltd	3 6	3D, 5	
Tyneside Tramways and Tramroads Co	4 8½	3D, OT30	Headlights on upper dash and vestibuled
Volks Electric Tramway	2 8½		
Wakefield and District Light Railways	4 8½	3R, 9R	
Wallesey Corporation Tramways	4 8½	8D	
Walsall Corporation Tramways	3 6	8R, 9D, BT44	Remove upper deck quarterlights from BT44
Walthamstow Corporation Tramways	4 8½	3D, 4D, 7, 12	
Warrington Corporation Tramways	4 8½	3D, 11D	11D add upper deck covered ends from Kit 2
Wednesbury Corporation Tramways	3 6	3R, 8D, 11R	
Wemyss and District Tramways Co Ltd	3 6		
West Bromwich Corporation Tramways	3 6	3D, 5, 8D, 9D	
West Ham Corporation Tramways	4 8½	2D, 3D, 4D, 12	
West Hartlepool Corporation Tramways	3 6	5	
Weston Super Mare & District Electric Supply Co Ltd	4 8½	8R	
Wigan Corporation Tramways	3 6	3R	
Wigan Corporation Tramways	4 8½	3R, 4D, BT33	

System	Gauge	Kits	Notes
	ft in		
Wolverhampton Corporation Tramways	3 6	3D, 3R	
Wolverhampton District Electric Tramways Ltd	3 6	3D, 5, 8D	
Worcester Electric Traction Co Ltd	3 6	8D	
Wrexham & District Electric Tramways Ltd	3 6	8R	
York Corporation Tramways	3 6	3D	
Yorkshire West Riding Electric Tramways Ltd	4 8½	3R, 9R	
Yorkshire Woollen District Tramways	4 8½	3R	

Appendix 2

Manufacturers of toy and model trams worldwide

I am indebted to Geoff Price for his help in compiling this list. It is not complete and I doubt that a full listing of all the tram models and toys which have ever been produced will be compiled by anyone. However, I hope I have managed to get all the more common and famous examples in the list and the majority of the more obscure ones.

A Toys, Portugal—Tin plate toy made circa 1940. Tramcar.

Amsterdam Tramway Company, Holland—Card cut out. Amsterdam tram No 780.

Anbrico, UK—White metal kits OO gauge. Sheffield Roberts. Bradford balcony. BT33—Balcony tram, 3 windows upper and lower saloon; BT43—Balcony tram, 4 windows upper and 3 lower saloons; BT44—Balcony tram, 4 windows upper and lower saloon; CT33—Enclosed tram, 3 windows upper and lower saloon; CT43—Enclosed tram, 4 windows upper and 3 lower saloons; CT44—Enclosed tram, 4 windows upper and lower saloon; CT44B—Enclosed tram, 4 windows upper and lower saloon, destination box variation; OT30—Open-top tram, 3 window; OT40—Open-top tram, 4 window; TT50—Toast-rack, 50 seats.

Arcade, USA—Cast iron made circa 1935. Trolley car No 14.

Arnold, W. Germany—Motorised ready-made model N gauge. 2960—MAN/Simmering tram, Salzburg SVB red livery; 2963—MAN/Simmering tram, DR green livery; 2972—Matching trailer, Salzburg SVB; 2973—Matching trailer, DR.

Associated Hobby Manufacturers (AHM), USA—Motorised ready made model HO gauge (manufactured by Mehanotehnika in Yugoslavia). 5301—Four-wheel Birney Trolley in six liveries: B, Public Service Company; C, Municipal Railway; D, PTC; E, Connecticut Company; F, United Transit Lines; G, Third Avenue Railway System; 5302—Boeing Light Rail Articulated Vehicle in two liveries: 02—Boston Transit Authority; 03—San Francisco Municipal Railway.

Bachmann, USA—Motorised ready-made model HO gauge, manufactured in Hong Kong. 1310—Brill bogie trolley, Market Street; 1311—Brill bogie trolley, PRT; 1312—Brill bogie trolley, South Shore Line; 1315—Brill bogie trolley, South Hills Lines.

Beamish North of England Open Air Museum, UK—Card cut out. Gateshead tram No 10.

Bec Kits, UK—White metal kits, OO gauge for the UK models and HO for the Continental models. 1—Stores van, snowbroom, snowplough; 2—Enclosed top, LCC type; 3—Open-top, 3-window; 4—Balcony top, 3 windows upper and lower saloon; 5—Uncanopied open-top, 3-window; 6—Open-top, 6-window; 7—Balcony top, 6 windows upper and lower saloon; 8—Open-top, 4-window; 9—Balcony top, 4 windows upper and lower saloon; 10—Leeds Horsfield; 11—Balcony top, 4-window upper saloon and 3 lower saloon; 12—Bogie, Classes E and E/1; 14—London and Leeds Feltham; 15—Glasgow Standard; 19—PCC street car; 22—Hamburg Z1 triebwagen; 23—Hamburg Z2 triebwagen; 24—Hamburg Z2B beiwagen; 25—Hawa triebwagen; 26—Hawa beiwagen; 28—Hamburg V2; 29—Hamburg V6E; 30—Den Haag PCC 1100 series; 31—Brussels PCC 7000 series (Hamburg 3060).

Bing, Germany—Tinplate models made between 1900 and 1925. Various British and Continental types of tram and trailer, single- and double-deck, in various model railway scales and gauges.

Bowser, USA—Cast metal kits, HO gauge; PCC trolley; Brill suburban bogie car; Indiana Railroad high speed car; Jewett Liberty Belle; Jewett style freelance.

Brawa, W. Germany—Motorised ready-made model in HO gauge. 455—Three small works trailers; 456—Diesel tramway/railway works vehicle, Motorised ready-made model N gauge; 1125—Motor car for tramcar 3-car set; 1126—Rear motor car for above; 1127—Centre trailer unit for above.

BS, ?—Tinplate tram and trailer clockwork set.

Bournemouth Passenger Transport Association, UK—White metal kit, 00 gauge. 1—Bournemouth tram No 60, ex-Poole tram No 6.

Carette, Germany—Tinplate trams and trailers made from the late 1800s until the 1930s. They were made in the popular model railway gauges of the time. The range included: 1090/10—Tram and trailer; 1091/10—Tram and trailer.

Carlisle & French, USA—Tinplate models made from the late 1800s until the 1930s. They were made in the popular model railway gauges of the time. A range of various types was available.

William J. Clouser, USA—Tram bodies in epoxy resin castings, O gauge. North Shore Coach; North Shore Combine.

CM, Hong Kong—Plastic friction-drive toys. 504—Double-deck 4-wheel car; 510—Hong Kong double-deck tram, green; 547—Double-deck 4-wheel car.

Coelho de Sousa, Portugal—Tinplate toys made in the 1950s. 4-wheel push-along in blue and green.

Copetown Car Works, USA—Diecast kits in O gauge. A variety of types were made including: Philadelphia Rapid Transit 'Hog Island' cars.

Corrocraft Jewellery, UK—Charm for bracelet. 3700/06—Gold-plated single-deck trolley car.

CP, Portugal—Tinplate toys. Tramcar, type not known; City of Braga tram.

Craftmaster, USA—Wooden kit, year of manufacture not known. San Francisco horse tram.

Cromer, UK—White metal kit in N gauge, now being made by Thameshead Transport Kits. Brill open-top 4-wheel tram.

Custom Brass, USA—Motorised ready-made trams in brass, HO gauge. The range included: Metropolitan Street Railway trolleycar; TARS DT trolleycar.

Daiya, Japan—Tinplate toy. 7021—Tram in cream livery.

D&M, UK—White metal kit in N gauge. Double-deck freelance tram to fit a Lima chassis.

Devon Pottery, UK—Novelty pottery tramcar.

Dinky Toys, UK—Diecast toy made just before the war. 27—Double-deck bogie tram (possibly LCC 1).

Doll, Germany—Tinplate trams and trailers made to the popular model railway scales of the time. Made approximately between 1918 and 1940. A range of different types and various scales were made.

Doyusha, Japan—Plastic ready-made models in N gauge. Tokyo tram; Kyoto tram.

DRGM, Germany—Tinplate toy made circa 1920; 345—Stocktram.

Egger Bahn, W. Germany—Motorised ready-made model in HOe (narrow gauge). Steam tram *Fiery Elias*; bogie coach to suit.

Espewe, East Germany—Plastic toys, date of manufacture not known. Tram and trailer.

Fairfield Traction Models, USA—Motorised ready-made models in brass, HO gauge. Included in the range made are: Brooklyn 8000; Chicago Pullman; Chicago Broadway; Chicago Broadway one-man car; Pittsburg double-ended car; Pittsburg single-ended car.

H. Fischer & Company, Germany—Tinplate toy made circa 1920. Toonerville trolley.

Forster, UK—Novelty stoneware. Nottingham single-deck tram No 213.

FP, Portugal—Wooden toy made circa 1950. Oporto tram.

Ginga, Japan—Ready-made model in HO gauge. Tokyo tram (Toden) type 600.

GOG Tram, W. Germany—Motorised ready-made models in HO gauge. Old time tram with clerestory in various colours; Old time trailer with clerestory in various colours; Modern tram in various colours; Modern trailer in various colours; Bogie cars in various liveries and changes in style.

Gozan, Spain—Tinplate and plastic toy. 15—Tramcar *Tranuitin*.

Grip, E. Germany—Tinplate and plastic toys sold under the name Trambino. Clockwork tram and trailer with an oval of track. Yellow and green liveries. Friction push-along tram of the same design.

Guntermann, Germany—Tinplate trams made 1910 to circa 1930. The range included single- and double-deck cars in various sizes.

Guinness, UK—Promotional tram in metal made circa 1960.

Hallmark, USA—C&CE *Red Rail* Trolley.

Hamo, W. Germany—Motorised ready-made models in HO gauge. 150—4-wheel, short clerestory; 205—4-wheel, short clerestory; 206—4-wheel, long clerestory; 126—Bogie, no pantograph; 127—Bogie, with pantograph; 250—4-wheel trailer, no clerestory; 252—4-wheel trailer, long clerestory; 129—Bogie trailer; 130—Works truck; 131—Works sand wagon; 132—Bogie works rail wagon; 204—4-wheel, old time car; 203—4-wheel trailer, old time car.

Hanse Toys, Sweden—Wooden toy made circa 1930. 703—Tramcar Kobenhavns Spoveje.

Harris Edge, UK—Card cut out model. Brush open-top 4-wheel car of 1914.

Hawk, USA—Plastic kit to O gauge. San Francisco cable car, now produced by Testors.

Historic Commercial Vehicle Club, UK—Card kit. London United Tramways T type. BTC Tramcar.

Hobbies, UK—Wooden kit, a less elaborate fretwork type construction. 246—London West Ham tram.

Huntley, Boorne & Stevens, UK—Tinplate container sometimes in the form of a money box. London electrical tram.

Images d'Epinal, France—Paper kit. Tram.

Indianapolis Car Company, USA—Motorised ready-made models in epoxy resin to O gauge. The range includes: ICC 429 Clouser cars.

Iron Art, USA—Cast iron reproduction trams using Arcade patterns. 334—Trolley car No 14.

Johill Company, UK—Toy trams in tinplate and diecast. Kingsway subway car, tinplate; London tram route 33, diecast.

JAS, Portugal—Tinplate toy made circa 1950. Tramcar.

JH, Germany—Tinplate toy. Tram set with rails, clockwork.

Katsumi Models, Japan—Motorised ready-made models in HO gauge, including: Old Tokyo tram, 1930s type.

Kawai, Japan—Motorised ready-made model in HO gauge. Kobe city tram.

Keyser (K's), UK—White metal kits in OO gauge. Metropolitan Electric Tramways E type; Wisbech & Upwell steam tram (LNER, ex-GE).

Ken Kidder, Japan—Motorised ready-to-run models in HO gauge, many brass models of USA tramcars. Also a plastic model: Suburban bogie car.

David O. King Inc, USA—Motorised ready-made car in O gauge. 3—San Francisco cable car, 4-wheel, 3-rail.

Kingsbury, USA—Pressed metal toy. Peter Witt streetcar.

L Toys, Hong Kong—Plastic toy. 547—Double-deck tram.

La Belle, USA—A range of USA traction kits in HO gauge, including: 51 ft interurban No 82; 51 ft interurban; 60 ft interurban combine; 64 ft interurban combine; 51 ft interurban WD; interurban coach; Buffalo, Rochester & Lockport coach; Buffalo, Rochester & Lockport combine; Sacramento Northern coach; Sacramento Northern combine; 4-door freight motor.

Lehmann, Germany—Plastic toy. 970—Push-along toy 'Gnomy' tram; 971—Matching trailer. Motorised ready-made models (LGB) in large scale on narrow gauge track. Steam tram; 4-wheel unvestibuled tram with pantograph; 4-wheel unvestibuled tram with bow; 4-wheel matching trailer.

Lesney, UK—Diecast, Models of Yesteryear. London County Council E/1 type.

Lilliput, Austria—Motorised ready-made model in HO gauge. Vienna 4-wheel tram in various colours; Vienna 4-wheel trailer in matching colours.

Lilliput Miniatures, UK—Card cut out OO gauge. London Transport tram.

Lionel, USA—Motorised ready-made models in O gauge. This famous model railway manufacturer added a number of trams, trolleys and interurbans to their catalogue in the 1920s and 30s.

Locomotive Workshop, USA—Motorised ready-made models in O gauge. The range includes: Birney car; Interurban; Single-ended Peterwitt car; Double-ended Peterwitt car; PCC.

Mabmapt, Russia—Tinplate tramcar.

Machin, UK—Open-top Sheffield tram No 123; Horse-drawn Sheffield tram No 9.

Manurba, USA—Tramcar and trailer.

G. Mark, Japan—Plastic kits in O gauge, all based on Japanese trams. 1—Single-deck tram; 2—Single-deck tram; 3—Single-deck tram, Tokyo City; 4—Double-deck tram, Osaka.

Marklin, Germany—Tinplate models added to the range of model railway items pre-1930. There were a variety of models and sizes.

Mar Toys, UK—Tinplate toy. Mountaineer tramcar.

Mar Toys, USA—Tinplate toy. Rapid transit car.

Terry Martin, UK—White metal and etched zinc kits in OO gauge. Bellamy top deck for converting Bec Kits, white metal; Liverpool cabin car, etched zinc; Liverpool 770 series, etched zinc.

Meadowcroft Models, UK—Motorised ready-made brass trams in O and OO gauge. A wide variety of models were made. Also a similar range of brass kits in OO gauge.

Meccano, France—Construction kit made in the 1930s. Tramway Macanique.

Mehanotehnika, Yugoslavia—Motorised ready-made models in HO gauge, also sold under AHM & Model Power. 4-wheel Birney car in various liveries; 4-wheel trailer to suit; Boeing articulated rapid transit car in two liveries.

Micromodels, UK—Card cut out kits. Blackpool Coronation car; London United open-top tramcar; North London steam tram; London horse tram.

Modelbau Bader, Switzerland—Various kits in HO including: Swiss standard tramcar.

Modelcraft, UK—Plans for making your own kit in OO gauge. EA137—BTH open-top tramcar; EA138—Blackpool double-deck tramcar.

Model Power, Canada—Motorised ready-made models in HO gauge, manufactured by Mehanotehnika. Birney 4-wheel car, Toronto; Birney 4-wheel car, Downtown.

Model Traction Supply, USA—White metal kits HO gauge. Flat bed works car; Flat bed works car with cabs; Differential dump car. Ready-made range of epoxy resin cars including: CNS&M 128-141 Class interurban; CTA 4000 series; NYW&B coach; Indiana Railway subway car; CTA 1-50 series rapid transit.

Model Tramcar Design, UK—Etched brass kits in OO gauge. 1—Blackpool toast-rack; 2—Blackpool pantograph car; 3—Blackpool standard, balcony version; 4—Blackpool standard, balcony version; 4—Blackpool Marton Vambac; 5— Blackpool open boat car.

Model Tramway System, USA—Ready-made models in brass to HO gauge, including: Berlin Class T24, tram and trailer.

Munson Books, UK—Card cut out tram. Kilmarnock bogie car, 1928 type.

Nacoral, Spain—Battery-operated plastic toy. Tramcar Tranvia Escolar.

Nickel Plate Products, USA—Motorised ready-made brass models in HO gauge, the range includes: South Shore coach; South Shore combine; Liberty liner; Electroliner; South Shore 700 Class; Milwaukee EF3-5.

Nitto Kagaku, Japan—Plastic kit including display case. Horse tram.

Novus, UK—Card cut out kit in OO gauge. Birmingham balcony car No 395.

Oroba, Germany—Clockwork tinplate toy. Double-deck tram.

Pacific Traction, USA—San Diego Class 5 Series 400 streetcar, O gauge brass model.

Parks, Hong Kong—Plastic toy copy of the Lesney Model of Yesteryear tramcar. 717—London County Council Class E/1.

Pathesiza, Greece—Plastic toy. 163—Tramcar.

Payva, Spain—Tinplate and plastic friction-drive toy. 87—Tramcar.

Penny Toys, Germany—Tinplate toy. Tramcar.

Platignum, UK—Card cut out kit as part of a self-colouring kit. Tramcar 1922 type.

Playskool, Germany—Le Tramway, San Francisco No 504.

Pliz, UK—Nickel silver kits, including: Leeds Middleton bogie car; Liverpool Green Goddess; Manchester single-deck bogie car.

Polks, USA—Ready-made model in HO gauge. Brill car.

Q-car, USA—Moulded epoxy resin tramcar bodies in HO gauge to fit on: Bowser chassis; Brooklyn PCC; St Louis PCC.

Radar, Portugal—Plastic toy, a copy of the early version of the Wiking model. Tramcar.

Ribeiro, Portugal—Tinplate toy made pre-1940. Tramcar.

Rico, Spain—Tinplate toy made circa 1920. Tramcar.

Rivarossi, Italy—Ready-made tramway system in HO gauge. Rome 4-wheel tram with trolley pole, green livery; matching trailer; Rome 4-wheel tram with bow collector, yellow livery; matching trailer.

Roco, Austria—Ready-made models in HO gauge. 8500—Cologne Duwag 6-axle articulated tram; 8501—Karlsruhe Duwag 6-axle articulated tram; 8502—Albtalbahn Duwag 6-axle articulated tram; 8504A—Cologne Duwag 8-axle articulated tram.

Terry Russell, UK—A range of O gauge and $\frac{3}{8}$ in drawings and also many parts for O gauge modellers including motorised trucks: C2—EMB Hornless 9 ft w/b; C3—Brill 22E max trac; C4—Brill 21E 8 ft w/b; C5—M&G max trac; C6—EE equal wheel; C7—London equal wheel; C9—EMB lightweight; C10—Brill 21E 6 ft w/b; C11—EMB max trac; C12—Peckham Cantilever 6 ft 6 in; C13—Brill 27G equal wheel; C14—Brill 39E reversed max trac; C15—Peckham P22 8 ft 6 in; C16—Peckham P35 8 ft 6 in; C17—EMB heavyweight; C18—Maley & Taunton swing link; C19—EE Blackpool; C20—Melbourne & Metropolitan Tramways 15A bogie; C21—Hurst Nelson LCC Class 5; C22—EMB heavyweight; C23—Brill 79e Birney; C24—Baldwin TCL66.

Sanchis, Spain—Tinplate and plastic toys. PCC streetcar various colours.

Sharps Toffees, UK—Promotional tinplate toy made circa 1930. Tramcar, toffee tin with added truck and wheels.

S.V. Shaw, Canada—Wood and wickerwork toy made in the late 1800s. Horse-drawn tramcar.

Siku, Germany—Plastic toys, push along. V40—4-wheel tramcar with pantograph; V57—4-wheel trailer.

SNCO, Japan—San Francisco cable car.

S Soho, USA—Ready-made motorised tramcars in HO gauge. The range includes: Birney; North Shore 450 steeple cab; Portland Railway 1400 steeple cab; Los Angeles streetcar B1; Los Angeles streetcar B8; Los Angeles streetcar H1; Los Angeles streetcar H2; Los Angeles streetcar K; Los Angeles streetcar L; Los Angeles streetcar M1.

Stadium, Germany—Tinplate toy. Streetcar.

Suydam, Japan—Brass parts and ready-made motorised trams in HO gauge including: ITS Class C; ITS Class B; P&F 414; P&F 530; P&F 1000; P&F 1100; P&E 1200; P&E 1222; P&E 1252; P&E 1299; P&E 1372; P&E 1451; Pacific Electric Blimp 71 ft; Pacific Electric Blimp 67 ft; Pacific Electric Commodore business car; Pacific Electric Ten 55 ft coach; Pacific Electric Long Beach; Pacific Electric Ten 55 ft combine; Pacific Electric RPO box motor; Pacific Electric OB157 line car; Pacific Electric Express box motor; PCC doubled ended car; Steeple cab 1624.

Swedtram Aktiebolag, Sweden—Metal kits in HO gauge including: Goteborgs Sparvagar 1902 M1, S2 & S3; Goteborgs Sparvagar 1921 M5; Goteborgs Sparvagar 1928 S8; Kobenhavns Sporveje 1909; Malmo Stads Sparvagar 1925 F type; Kobenhavns Sparvagar 1930 Lundig M; Kobenhavns Sparvagar 1930

Lundig S; Kobenhavns Sparvagar 1942 M; Kobenhavns Sparvagar 1942 S; Kobenhavns Sparvagar 1909 M; Kobenhavns Sparvagar 1912 S; Stockholms Sparvagar 1926 A1; Stockholms Sparvagar 1922 B17; Oslo Sparvagar Hawa 1921 M; Oslo Sparvagar Hawa 1921 S; Odense Elektriske Sporvej ASEA 1911 M; Odense Elektriske Sporvej ASEA 1911 S; Goteborgs Sparvagar 1927 M9; Goteborgs Sparvagar 1930 S9; Goteborgs Sparvagar 1931 S10; Goteborgs Sparvagar 1908 M4; Goteborgs Sparvagar M25, M28, M29 and PCC; Stockholms Sparvagar 1944 A24; Stockholms Sparvagar 1944 B24; Kobenhavns Sporveje 1960 Duwag Articulated; Kolner Verkehrsbetriebe 1973 Stadtbahnwagen Type B Articulated.

Joseph Terry & Sons, UK—Promotional small box with little bars of chocolate. Single-deck 3-axle tram.

Testors, USA—Plastic kit in O gauge, orginally produced by Hawk Kits. San Francisco cable car.

Thameshead Transport Kits, UK—White metal kit in N gauge, originally produced by Cromer. 78—Brill open-top 4-wheel tram.

TM, Japan—Tinplate clockwork toy. 9232—Turntable tramway.

Tomica, Japan—Diecast model. San Francisco cabie car.

Tramway Museum Society, UK—Card cut out kit. Leicester car No 76.

Tranvia, Mexico—Plastic toy with brass wheels. Mexico City tram.

Trix, UK—Card cut out kit in O gauge, pre-cut. Brush open-top 4-wheel tram.

Tyco, USA—Ready-made motorised model in plastic, made to HO gauge. Various liveries including: Brill single-deck car—Main Street; Brill single-deck car—Nob Hill; Brill single-deck car—Broadway.

A.J. Van Riemsdyk, Holland—Ready-made metal models, motorised in O gauge. The range includes: double-deck trams in various styles; Belgian type single-deck tram; Matching trailer.

Jim Varney, UK—White metal kits in OO gauge. GF Train horse tram; LCC horse tram; Southampton Dome; Leeds car ex-Southampton Dome; Liverpool Green Goddess; Glasgow Goddess ex-Liverpool; London Transport E/3 or HR2.

VEB, E. Germany—Plastic toys about TT gauge. Horse tram; Electric tram; Matching trailer.

Walthers, USA—Model kits in metal and wood made to HO scale, the range includes: Birney Safety Car, 4-wheel (all metal kit); North Shore coach.

Western Railcraft, USA—Metal and wood kits in N gauge. North Shore coach; North Shore combine; Steeple Cab locomotive; Pacific Electric box motor; Pacific Electric coach; Pacific Electric combine.

Wiking, W. Germany—Plastic models all advertised as HO gauge, however 740 and 741 are nearer TT gauge. 69—Strassenbahn tram; 69a—Matching trailer; 740—Modern bogie tram; 741—Matching trailer.

Winty Toys, Hong Kong—Plastic toy. Horse tram.

Wuppertal, W. Germany—Card cut out. Hanging tramcar (Monorail).

Yodel, Japan—Ready-made motorised plastic model 9 mm gauge. Kyoto tram. Tokyo tram.

Yone, Japan—Tinplate clockwork toy. Tram.

ZAX, Italy—Tinplate toy. 523—Tram.

Manufacturer not known, *Hong Kong:* Plastic clockwork toy, trade mark child caricature with small C. 3612 Drin; Drinn tram. *UK:* Tin container with hinged lid. Tram No 342 to City Centre.

Appendix 3

Where to see trams in the British Isles

Operating systems*

Black Country Museum: Tipton Road, Dudley, West Midlands.
Blackpool Borough Transport, Electric Tramway: Blundell Street, Blackpool, Lancs.
Douglas Corporation Horse Tramways: Strathallan Crescent, Douglas, Isle of Man.
East Anglia Transport Museum: Chapel Road, Carlton Colville, Nr Lowestoft, Suffolk.
Great Orme Tramway (cable): Victoria Station, Church Walks, Llandudno, Gwynedd.
Manchester Transport Museum Society: Heaton Park Tramway, Manchester.
Manx Electric Railway: Strathallan Crescent, Douglas, Isle of Man.
National Tramway Museum: Crich, Matlock, Derbyshire.
North of England Open Air Museum: Beamish Hall, Stanley, Co Durham.
Seaton and District Electric Tramway: Harbour Road, Seaton, Devon.
Snaefell Mountain Railway: Laxey, Isle of Man.
Telford Town Tramway (steam): Telford Park, Telford, Salop.
Tyne and Wear Metro: Tyne and Wear PTE, Cuthbert House, All Saints, Newcastle upon Tyne.
Volks Electric Railway: Brighton, E Sussex.

The Blackpool Tramway nearing the end of a busy season, balloon car No 717 heads for the pleasure beach (photo D. Voice).

Above left *Getting ready to take out the first tram of the day on the Douglas Corporation Horse Tramway* (photo D. Voice).

Above *On the Manx Electric Railway a tramcar and trailer waits at Laxey for a Snaefell Tram prior to making a run to Douglas* (photo D. Voice).

Left *The single-deck Gateshead tram takes on passengers at the North of England Open Air Museum* (photo D. Voice).

Left *To the surprise and delight of holiday-makers and locals alike, Bolton No 66 ran in service at Blackpool during the 1981 season. Naturally it proved an attraction to tram-minded societies, who hired it for special trips. On this occasion the Transport Group of the Black Country Museum foresake their Dudley and Stourbridge tram for a run over the full Blackpool system* (photo D. Voice).

Static tram displays*

Belfast Transport Museum: Witham Street, Newtownards Road, Belfast.

Bradford Industrial Museum: Moorside Mills, Moorside Road, Bradford.

Bournemouth Transport Museum: Mallard Road Depot, Mallard Road, off Castle Lane, Bournemouth.

Douglas Horse Tram Display: Horse Tram Depot, Strathallan Crescent, Douglas, Isle of Man.

Edinburgh Transport Museum: Shrubhill Depot, Leith Walk, Edinburgh.

Glasgow Transport Museum: 25 Albert Drive, Glasgow.

Hull Transport Museum: 36 High Street, Kingston upon Hull, Humberside.

Manx Electric Railway Museum: Ramsey, Isle of Man.

Museum of Science and Industry: Newhall Street, Birmingham.

Science Museum: Exhibition Road, South Kensington, London.

*The opening days and hours of these tramways and museums do vary considerably. Some are very restricted, perhaps only opening a few days a year. Do check before visiting, particularly if a long journey is needed to reach the site.

Appendix 4

Miscellaneous information

Societies

Tramway and Light Railway Society—The society caters for people who have an interest in tramways and light railways from historic, modelling, research and general viewpoints. The society has a large scale model tramway layout, all modelled to the scale of ¼ in to 1 ft. The trams are miniatures of the vehicles which travelled the streets of Britain. There are also other active groups who model in smaller scales, including OO, HO and N gauges. The society publishes literature and photographs to help the modeller. There is also a diary of regular meetings. Further information is available from: Tramway and Light Railway Society, 6 The Woodlands, Brightlingsea, Colchester, Essex.

The Light Rail Transit Association—This society, formerly called the Light Railway Transport League, was founded in 1937 for the retention and development of tramways and light railways. It is an international body, well known for its support of LRT (light rail transit) and upgraded tramways—the intermediate mode between bus and metro. New members are welcomed, whether they be technical officers in the transport industry or interested amateurs. Members receive *Modern Tramway* by post each month and can buy major new LRTA books at reduced rates (the LRTA is an active publishing body). Regular meetings are held in many centres and the LRTA arranges study tours. Members can subscribe to *Tramway Review* at reduced price. Further information is available from: Light Rail Transit Association, 6 Hermitage Woods Crescent, St. John's, Woking, Surrey.

The Tramway Museum Society—This society runs Britain's National Tramway Museum at Crich, Derbyshire, where there are some 40 trams (horse, steam and electric) dating from 1873 to 1953. Most are restored and are operated in turn. An Edwardian street scene is being built around the tramway. The society also collects archival material—photos, documents, etc, and small items of historical research and eventual display. The museum depends for its continuation on its volunteer working members but it welcomes anyone to membership, whether they can help actively or not. Membership gives free entry and free riding at Crich, with reciprocal arrangements at some other museums, and a copy of the quarterly *Journal*. Further information is available from Tramway Museum Society, 49 Allman Road, Erdington, Birmingham.

Electric tramcar kit manufacturers

Anbrico Scale Models: Perseverance Street, Pudsey, West Yorkshire.
Bec Kits: PO Box 5, Aldershot, Hants.
Model Tramcar Design: Raymond Collins, 1st Floor, 26 Brown Street, Manchester, M2 1DN.

Overhead system and tram parts

R. Meadowcroft Models: 277 Keighley Road, Colne, Lancs.

Destinations, advertisements and other transfers

Mabex Products: 31 Pevensey Road, Eastbourne, Sussex.

O gauge tram parts

Terry Russell: Chaceside, St Leonards Park, Horsham, West Sussex.

Postcards

(Black and white)
W.J. Haynes: 18 Lamberts Field, Bourton on the Water, Glos.
(Colour and black and white)
Mumbles Railway Company: PO Box 79, Cheltenham Spa.
(Colour)
Prescott-Pickup & Co Ltd: 'Rodwin', Allscott, Telford, Salop, TF6 5EQ.

Books

The British Tram, by Frank E. Wilson.
British Tramway Guide, by P.H. Abell.
Current Collection for Tramway and Trolleybus Systems, by G.E. Baddeley and E.R. Oakley.
An Introduction to Tramway Modelling, (this book looks at modelling in ¾ in to the foot scale) by P. Hammond.
A Source Book Of Trams, by J.H. Price.
Trams in Colour Since 1945, by J. Joyce.
British Electric Tramcar Design 1885-1950, by R.W. Rush.

Index

Page numbers in italics refer to illustrations.

AHM, 19
Airfix kit conversions, 22-27, 32, *32*
Anbrico, 12, *43,* 46, 72, 190
Arnold, 18

Bachmann, 19
Bec Kits, 12, 14, 16, 17, 19, 33, 37-46, 47, 48, 66-72, 95, 190
Bing, *9,* 10, 11
Birmingham Corporation Trams, 7, *42,* 60, *61,* 62, 63
Birmingham Museum of Science and Industry, 9
Bispham to Little Bispham, 103, *103,* 104, *136, 162*
Blackpool Tramways; Jubilee Class, 86, *98,* 144; OMO, 168; Railgrinder, *21*; Standard, *75, 76*; Toast-rack, 55-59; Works cars, *21, 25*
Black Country Museum, *27, 28*
Bogies; Equal wheel, 47, 48, *52,* 53, 66; Maximum traction, 47, 66, *73*
Bolton Corporation, *73*
Bournemouth Passenger Transport Association, 14
Bowser, 19
Bracket Arm Traction Pole, 133
Brawa, 18
British United Tramways, 105, *105,* 106, *117*

Carette, 10
Carlisle and Finch, 10
Change pit, *124,* 129
Chassis, 22, *28,* 30, 35, 43, 44,

51, *52,* 53, 56, 57, 92, *93*
Clapham Tram Depot, *151,153*
CM, 15
Conduit System, 129, 130
Crich, see National Tramway Museum
Cromer Models, 14
Croydon Corporation Tramways, *36,* 37-42

D and M, 14
Dashes, 25
Dating buildings, 155, 157
Depots, 144-154
Dinky, *10,* 11
Doll, 11
Driver, 36
Dudley and Stourbridge Tramways, *27,* 28, 29, *75, 76*

Ears, 133, 137, 139
Edge Lane Depot, 147, 148
Edward Exley, 12
Egger Bahn, 15, *16*
Elektrische Tramweg Maatshappij, 106, 107, *107, 145*
Equal wheel bogie, 47, 48, *52,* 53, 66
Etched brass kits, 56-59
Experimental Feltham Tram-cars, 63, 65

Freelance British Style Tram, 27-32
Freelance works car, 22-27
Frogs (overhead), 133, 140, *140,* 141, *141,* 142
Fyldental Bahn, 107, 108, *108*

Glazing, 35, 36, 45, 50, 51, 63
Glossary, 166, 167
Gog tram, 17

Green Goddess, 47-55

Hamo, 12, 15, *17,* 119, 135
Handrails, 44, *44,* 45, *45*
Hangers, 133
Headlights, 25, 92
Historic Commercial Vehicle Club, 14
Hobbies, 15
Horse trams, 9, *13,* 14

Johill, 12
Joints for overhead wire, 142

Ken Kidder, 19
Keyser, 13, *13*
Kidderminster and Stourport Electric Tramways, 144
Kinver Light Railway, 144

Layout design, 99-115
Lesney, 11
Lettering, 43, 83, *84,* 85
Lifeguards, 36, 45, 71, 72, 97
Light Rail Transit Association, 37, 74, 189
Lilliput, 16
Lining, 70, 82, 83
Link, Roy, 15
Lionel, 10
Liverpool Corporation Tramways; Edge Lane Depot, 147, 148; Green Goddess, 47-55
Loughborough Model Shop, 120
Low relief buildings, 158-161

Mabex transfers, 45, 97, 98, 190
Mark, 20
Marklin, 10
Martin, Terry, 14
Masking techniques, 50

Maximum traction bogie, 47, 66, *73*
Meadowcroft Models, 12, 135, *136*, 137, 140, 190
Mehanotehnika, 19, 27-32, 92, *93*
Metropolitan Electric Tramways No 331, 63-72
Micro Models, 14
Model Power, 19
Model Traction Supply, 19, 59
Model Tramcar Design, 14, 19, 55-59, 190
Mumbles Railway Company, 89, 190

Narrow Gauge Steam Tramway, 104, *104*, *164*
National Tramway Museum, 15, 56, 59, 73, 74, *152*
Negative drawing techniques, 62, 67, 88, 89, 90
N gauge rapid transit, *100*
Novus, 15

Overhead wire, 139-142

Painting techniques, 39, 77-82
Panelling techniques, 83, *83*
Pantographs, 87, 95
Passenger carrying model tramcar, *96*
Passengers, 36, 45, 46, *46*, 51, *52*, 53, 59, 71
People, 163, *164*, 165
Philadelphia turning circle, *113*
Picardy Council Tramways,

102, *102*, 103, *159*, 162, *163*
Pinto collection, 9
Points, *117*, 123, 125, 126
Pontevedro, 111, *111*, 112
Preferred direction, 36
Protection for models, *84*, 85
Purley Depot, *150*

Research, 73-77
Rico, *10*
Rivarossi, 15, *18*, 31, *31*, *117*, 119, 135, *138*
Road surface, *117*, 118-123, *124*, 127, 129
Roco, 16
Roofs, 26, 36, 51, *75*, 93, 95
Russell, Terry, 89, 190

San Francisco Tram Models, *20*
Scrollwork, *134*, 137
Seaton and District Tramways, 144
Seats, 40, 41, *41*, *42*, 44, *58*, 59, *75*, 95
Self-etching primer, 59, 90
Sharps, 15
Sheffield Roberts, *43*, 46
Sherwood Tramways, 106, *106*, *118*, *152*
Shinohara track, 123
Soldering; Basic techniques, 68; White metal, 48
Span wire, 133
Stairs, 41
Steam trams, 9, 13, *13*, 15, *16*
Steps, 27
Stud contact system, *128*, 129

Suydam, 19, 137, 140
Swansea and Mumbles Railway, 86-98, 118, *152*
Swedtram Aktiebolag, 17

Tamebridge, *99*, 110, *110*, 111, *149*, *161*
Tenshodo Motor Unit, 12, 22
Terrys, 15
Thatchway Transit, 108, 109, *109*
Track, 116-131
Tram Sets, 15, *17*, *18*
Tramway and Light Railway Society, 6, 74, 189
Tramway Museum Society, 15, 74, 152, 189
Transfer making, 85
Traverser, 149-154
Trix, 15, *17*
Trolley poles; Open-top trams, *38*, 39, 40; Closed-top trams, 53, *54*, 55
Trolley reverser, *138*, *141*, 143

Varney, Transport Replicas, *13*, 14, 47-55
Vestibule construction, 60-63

Walthers, 18, 33-37
Windows, 35, 36, 45, 50, 51, 63
Wire mesh, 43
Wolverhampton Corporation Tramways, 96, 112, *112*, 113, *137*, *158*, *160*, 163, *164*
Wolverhampton and District Tramways, *42*
Works cars, *21*, *25*, 72
Wyking, 18